Sicily: Palermo & the Northwest

Mary-Ann Gallagher

Credits

Footprint credits

Editor: Alan Murphy
Production and layout: Jen Haddington
Maps: Gail Townsley

Managing Director: Andy Riddle
Content Director: Patrick Dawson
Publisher: Alan Murphy
Publishing Managers: Felicity Laughton, Jo Williams, Nicola Gibbs
Marketing and Partnerships Director: Liz Harper
Marketing Executive: Liz Eyles
Trade Product Manager: Diane McEntee
Account Managers: Paul Bew, Tania Ross
Advertising: Renu Sibal, Elizabeth Taylor
Finance: Phil Walsh

Photography credits
Front cover: Andrea Paggiaro/ Shutterstock
Back cover: Tonino Corso/ Shutterstock

Printed in Great Britain by CPI Antony Rowe, Chippenham, Wiltshire

Every effort has been made to ensure that the facts in this guidebook are accurate. However, travellers should still obtain advice from consulates, airlines, etc about travel and visa requirements before travelling. The authors and publishers cannot accept responsibility for any loss, injury or inconvenience however caused.

Publishing information
Footprint *Focus Sicily: Palermo & the Northwest*
1st edition
© Footprint Handbooks Ltd
March 2012

ISBN: 978 1 908206 49 7
CIP DATA: A catalogue record for this book is available from the British Library

® Footprint Handbooks and the Footprint mark are a registered trademark of Footprint Handbooks Ltd

Published by Footprints
6 Riverside Court
Lower Bristol Road
Bath BA2 3DZ, UK
T +44 (0)1225 469141
F +44 (0)1225 469461
footprinttravelguides.com

Distributed in the USA by Globe Pequot Press, Guilford, Connecticut

All rights reserved. No part of this publication may be reproduced, stored in a retrieval system, or transmitted, in any form or by any means, electronic, mechanical, photocopying, recording, or otherwise without the prior permission of Footprint Handbooks Ltd.

The content of Footprint *Focus Sicily: Palermo & the Northwest* has been extracted from Footprint's *Sicily* which was researched and written by Mary-Ann Gallagher.

- **5 Introduction**
  - 4 *Map: Sicily*

- **6 Planning your trip**
  - 6 Places to visit in Palermo and the Northwest
  - 8 Getting to Palermo and the Northwest
  - 9 Transport in Palermo and the Northwest
  - 11 Where to stay in Palermo and the Northwest
  - 14 Food and drink in Palermo and the Northwest
  - 16 Festivals in Palermo and the Northwest
  - 19 Essentials A-Z

- **23 Palermo and around**
  - **24 Palermo**
  - 26 *Map: Palermo*
  - 36 Palermo listings
  - **41 Around Palermo**
  - 49 Around Palermo listings

- **55 Western Sicily**
  - **56 Trapani and around**
  - 62 Trapani and around listings
  - **65 The Egadi Islands and Pantelleria**
  - 68 The Egadi Islands and Pantelleria listings

- **71 Southwestern Sicily**
  - **72 Marsala and around**
  - 77 Marsala and around listings
  - **80 Agrigento and around**
  - 86 Agrigento and around listings

- **89 Background**
  - 90 History

- **99 Footnotes**
  - 100 Menu reader
  - 102 Index

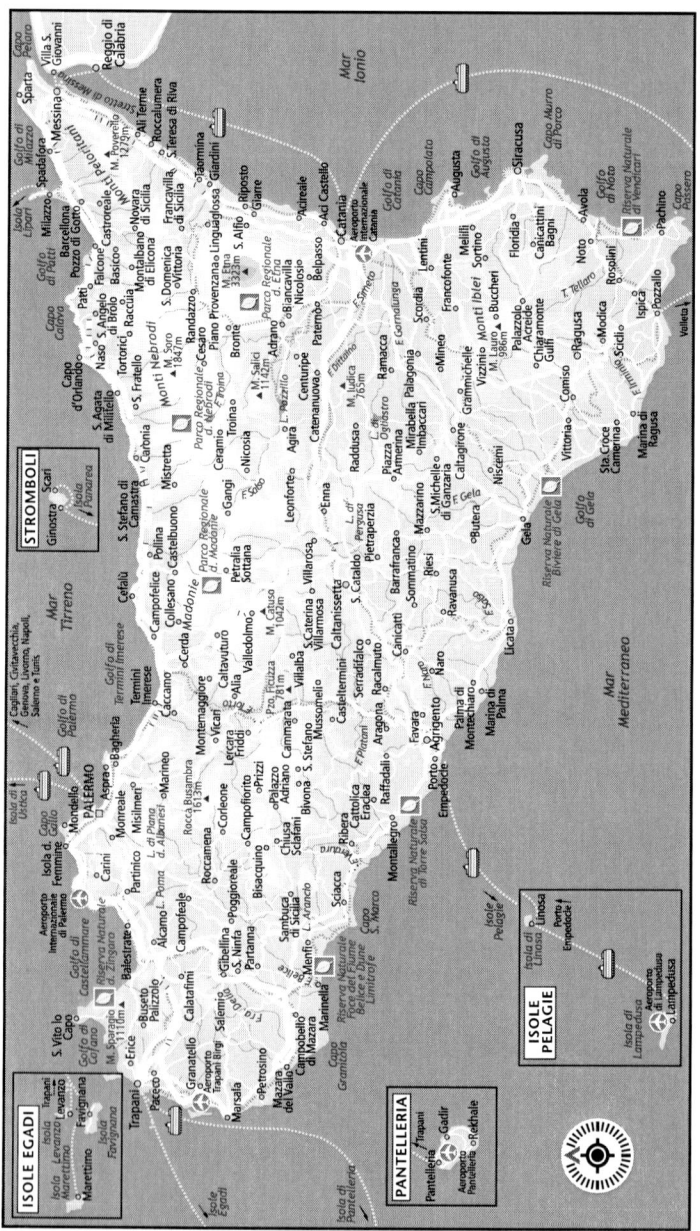

4 • Palermo & the Northwest

Sicily is a sly seductress. You'll fall for her – everyone does – but she won't make it easy. First impressions are intense, but paradoxical: beautiful and brutal, anarchic and serene, exuberant and insular, the island resists all easy definitions. Countless rulers have come and gone, each adding something different to the mix. The result is a complex yet infinitely beguiling land.

For the Greeks, Sicily was the island of Demeter, who endowed it with beauty and natural abundance. They built their cities as though their civilisation would last forever – even now, these ancient ruins are breathtaking. The subtle legacy of the Arabs is apparent in the islanders' hospitality and rich cuisine, and the glorious, golden cathedrals were bequeathed by the Normans. Tragically for Sicily, everyone else – from the Romans to the Bourbons – was out for what they could get. And what wasn't stripped out, was bombed to smithereens during the Second World War.

Grinding poverty, institutionalised corruption and the Cosa Nostra have taken a heavy toll. But there has been a renaissance in recent years: historic cities are being slowly restored; swathes of the glorious landscape are protected in nature reserves; and grassroots organisations have found the collective courage to stand up against the mafia. There's a heady sense of hope in the air – just one more reason to fall a little more in love.

This guide focuses on Palermo, the thrilling, chaotic Sicilian capital, with its battered *palazzi*, vibrant street markets and gilded Norman monuments. Around Palermo, we visit ancient ruins at Segesta, spectacularly unspoilt coastline at the Zingaro Reserve, and the idyllic seaside town of Cefalù. Then we travel west, visiting the whitewashed city of Trapani, set amid vast salt flats under a huge sky, the Egadi Islands and the far-flung celeb haunt of Pantelleria. We visit the wineries of Marsala, and the lively little port town of Mazara del Vallo, and then explore the finest surviving antique temple complex outside Greece in Agrigento.

Planning your trip

Places to visit in Palermo and the Northwest

Palermo and around
Palermo, Sicily's theatrical, bomb-blasted, anarchic capital, is tightly packed around a wide, curving bay. It was considered one of the loveliest cities of medieval Europe, but centuries of war, neglect and poverty have stripped it of much of its former beauty. Some spellbinding corners survive, particularly the glittering 12th-century Cappella Palatina, in the Palazzo dei Normanni (Norman Palace), one of the great jewels of Arabic-Norman art. There are some interesting museums, but much of the city's allure lies in exploring its crumbling alleys and squares, and visiting the eye-popping markets with their glistening offal and gaping fish. Palermo's seaside suburb, elegant Mondello, is dotted with pretty art nouveau villas submerged in greenery. On a hill overlooking the city, the magnificent cathedral of Monreale is encrusted with dazzling Byzantine mosaics. To the east, the once-chic resort of Bagheria is still scattered with extraordinary follies and whimsical turn-of-the-century villas. Much of Palermo province is former bandit country, and even now towns like Corleone and Prizzi summon up visions of the Mafia (however much they wish they didn't). Farther east is Cefalù, one of the prettiest seaside towns on the Mediterranean, with a red-roofed old quarter piled up beneath a cliff.

Western Sicily
The western coast of Sicily is flat and ethereal, the coastline delicately etched with the pale outline of salt pans. The provincial capital Trapani, with its surprisingly elegant old quarter and an excellent reputation for its cuisine, occupies a slender promontory. Nearby, the magical, medieval hill town of Erice clings to the mountain-top, overlooking the craggy San Vito Lo Capo and the superb Riserva Naturale dello Zingaro. This reserve encompasses a long swathe of deliciously unspoilt, craggy coastline, with hiking trails and tiny coves. Lost in the hills inland, the great Doric temple of Segesta, erected in the fifth century BC, is heart-stoppingly beautiful. Celebrities in search of peace and seclusion head for the tiny and enchanting island of Pantelleria, closer to Africa than Sicily. The trio of Egadi Islands are more accessible, and the fishing villages, striking coastline and rocky coves draw floods of summer visitors.

Southwestern Sicily
The west boasts two lively and appealing port towns: Marsala, famous for its delicious fortified wine, and Mazara del Vallo, which has an attractive old quarter. There are more spectacular ancient ruins at Selinunte, romantically located on a clifftop amid a profusion of wild flowers. The southern coast, an otherwise workaday region with gritty ports and low-key resorts, contains one of Sicily's headlining attractions: the stunning Valle dei Templi in Agrigento. This magnificent and extraordinarily well preserved temple group, dating back to the sixth to fifth centuries BC, is the finest to be found outside mainland Greece.

Best of Palermo and the Northwest

Palazzo dei Normanni and Cappella Palatina, Palermo Palermo's 12th-century Norman Palace, built by Roger II, contains one of the most dazzling yet intimate chapels to be found anywhere. Every surface is covered with shimmering mosaics, with bible stories and curious fables exquisitely rendered in miniature, and the ceiling and columns are masterfully worked in gilt and marble. Page 25.

Cattedrale di Monreale A glorious, golden cathedral crowns the serene hill town of Monreale, high above Palermo. Almost a thousand years ago, the finest Greek mosaicists, aided by their Sicilian pupils, transformed the interior into a breathtaking, gilded masterpiece, filling it with Byzantine mosaics of such beauty and grandeur that they rank among the finest in Europe. Page 43.

Cefalù A picture-postcard seaside village curled around the base of a dramatic headland, Cefalù has managed to retain oodles of old-fashioned charm despite the crowds that descend every summer. Chic Italians come for the fabulous beaches, but the ancient town has plenty more to offer – not least a splendid Norman cathedral containing superb Byzantine mosaics. Page 45.

Erice An ethereal, medieval town of cobbled streets and noble palaces, little Erice is perched so high on its hilltop that it often sits above the clouds. When they part, the views across the coastline far, far below are truly magnificent. Page 58.

Riserva Naturale dello Zingaro Much of the long, craggy finger of the Capo di San Vito is now a stunning nature reserve, offering one of the last unspoilt stretches of Mediterranean coastline. Scramble down to rocky coves of heart-stopping beauty and splash about in the impossibly blue sea. Page 59.

Segesta Travellers have long gasped at their first glimpse of Segesta, emerging like a mirage from a serene and verdant valley. The great temple has stood here for more than two and a half millennia. Above it, on a wind-whipped crag, are the remains of a Greek theatre with views across the hills. Page 59.

Pantelleria When celebs want to get away from it all in style, they come to the secretive little island of Pantelleria, which is geographically closer to Africa than Italy. The traditional *dammusi* (domed stone dwellings) that dot the hilly landscape now contain some of the most chic boutique accommodation to be found in the Mediterranean. Page 67.

Selinunte Perched magically on a remote, silent headland, Selinunte is among the most poignant ancient sites in Sicily. The soaring columns of its roofless temples and the overgrown tumble of stones are all that survive of what was once one of the most powerful Greek colonies on the island. Page 74.

Valle dei Templi, Agrigento The great Greek temples of ancient Akragas, magnificently silhouetted high on a ridge near the modern town of Agrigento, are the finest Doric temples to be found anywhere outside mainland Greece. They date back to the sixth and fifth centuries BC, when Akragas was at the height of its powers. Page 81.

Getting to Palermo and the Northwest

Air

From UK and Ireland There are three international airports in Sicily: Palermo, Catania and Trapani. Another airport, Comiso (near Ragusa), has been constructed, but has yet to open, and access roads have yet to be completed. **British Airways** flies directly from London Gatwick to Catania; **easyJet** operates direct services from London Gatwick to Palermo and Catania; **Ryanair** flies directly from London Luton to Trapani airport, and from London Stansted to Palermo. There are summer-only charter flights to Catania with **Avro** and **Thomas Cook**. **Alitalia** offers services from London Heathrow to Palermo and Catania via Rome or Milan.

From North America Eurofly/Meridiana operate direct flights in summer from New York (JFK) to Palermo Airport. **Delta, United, Continental, US Airways, Alitalia** offer direct flights from the US to mainland Italian airports. Canadian travellers will have to change in the US, or fly to another European city for a connection. **Alitalia** fly directly from Toronto to Rome.

From rest of Europe and mainland Italy Direct flights to Sicilian airports depart from most major European cities. These are operated by **Air Berlin, Brussels Airlines, easyJet, Ryanair, ThomasCook, Transavia, TUI,** and **Vueling**. Check the company websites and whichbudget.com for specific routes.

There are numerous flights from most mainland Italian airports (including Bologna, Florence, Milan, Palma, Pisa, Rome, Turin, Venice and Verona) with **Alitalia-Air One, Wind Jet, easyJet,** and **Ryanair**, and the joint company **Meridiana-Eurofly** (meridiana.it).

Airport information Catania Fontanarossa Airport ⓘ *T095-723 9111, aeroporto.catania.it*, 5 km southeast of the city, is connected to the central train station by AMT Alibus bus no 457 (0500-2400, every 20 minutes, €1). A metro line is under construction and scheduled to open in 2016. A taxi to the centre costs €20-25. There are also direct bus services to other towns on the east coast, including Syracuse and Taormina.

Palermo Falcone Borsellino Airport ⓘ *T091-7020273, gesap.it*, is at Punta Raisi, 35 km west of central Palermo. An airport bus departs every 30 minutes (0645-2400, €5.80, buy tickets onboard, journey time 55 minutes) for piazza Politeama and the train station in central Palermo. There is also an hourly train service, **Trinacria Express** ⓘ *0554-2205, €5.80, 55 mins*. Taxis cost €30-40.

Trapani Birgi Airport ⓘ *T0923-842502, airgest.it*, 15 km southeast of Trapani and 15 km north of Marsala, is a hub for budget airlines and the main gateway to western Sicily. There are bus links to Trapani (every 30 minutes, €4.50, journey time 25 minutes), to Agrigento (1-2 services daily, €10.60) and to Marsala (2-4 services daily, €3.50), as well as Palermo.

The islands of **Lampedusa** and **Pantelleria** (pantelleriairport.it) have small national airports (both managed by Palermo's Falcone Borsellino airport, T091-702 0619, enac-italia.it), used for summer flights.

Rail

You can travel with **Eurostar** (eurostar.com) from London to Paris, then take a TGV train to Milan where you should spend the night before picking up a train to Naples the next day. Direct trains depart from Naples for Catania, Siracusa and Palermo. The Paris–Rome sleeper service has been temporarily suspended; it should begin again in summer 2012. From Rome, there are direct services, including a sleeper train, to Catania, Siracusa and Palermo. Tickets at raileurope.com (T0870-584 8848), useful information at seat61.com. From destinations in the rest of Europe, there are also direct passenger trains to Milan and Rome where you can change for services to Sicily.

Road

Car It's a 2450-km journey from London to Messina, or about 25 hours of driving time. You could halve the drive by taking the ferry from Genoa or Livorno to Palermo (see above). **Autostrade** ⓘ *T840-042121 for road conditions, autostrade.it*, provides information on Italian motorways, while **Automobile Club Italiana** ⓘ *T803116, aci.it*, gives out general driving information.

Bus/coach Eurolines ⓘ *T087-17818178, eurolines.co.uk*, operates three services per week going from London Victoria to Naples (via Milan) with a travel time of around 35 hours. There are bus connections from Naples to several points in Sicily with **SAIS** ⓘ *T800-211020, saisautolinee.it*.

Sea

The main Sicilian ports are Messina (northeast), Palermo (northwest) and Trapani (west). Travel by ferry is usually comfortable, but often considerably pricier than a budget flight.

Ferry from mainland Italy Caronte ⓘ *T090-364601, carontetourist.it*, and **FS ferries**, run by Italian State Railways (ferroviedellostato.it) operate ferry (25 mins) and hydrofoil (15 minutes) services between Messina and Villa San Giovanni. They also run services to Salerno three times a day. **Tirrenia** ⓘ *T02-2630 2803, tirrenia.it*, and **SNAV** ⓘ *T081-428 5555, snav.it*, operate daily Naples–Palermo crossings (9 hrs 45 mins – 10½ hrs). SNAV also runs crossings between Civitavecchia (Rome) and Palermo (11 hours) and between Naples and the Aeolian Islands. **Grandi Navi Veloci** ⓘ *T010-209 4591, gnv.it*, run daily (excluding Sunday) services between Genoa and Palermo (via Livorno) (20 hours). Ustica operate summer-only hydrofoils from Naples to Trapani (6½ hrs) and Favignana (7 hrs). Tirrenia runs ferries between Cagliari (Sardinia) and Trapani (13 hours). **Grimaldi** ⓘ *T089-253202, grimaldi-lines.com*, operate several routes: Civitavecchia–Catania, Civitavecchia–Trapani, Salerno–Palermo, Tunis–Palermo, Tunis–Trapani, Malta–Catania.

Transport in Palermo and the Northwest

Getting around Sicily can be an adventure. Public transport is erratic, and you'll need patience and a whole sheaf of Plan Bs. Don't bother with a car if you are in Sicily on a city break (parking and driving are a nightmare in all Sicilian cities, particularly Palermo) but a car is essential to explore the hidden corners of this beautiful island. If you're spending time on Sicily's offshore islands, leave the car behind (there are strict restrictions on bringing vehicles to certain islands during the summer season). The best road maps for the island are published by Touring Club Italiano and Michelin.

Air

The islands of Lampedusa and Pantelleria have small airports, with regular flights from Palermo, Trapani and mainland Italian airports in summer.

Rail

Mainland Italy has an extensive and efficient rail network, but Sicily's is decidedly patchy. The train is worth taking between Palermo and Messina; between Trapani, Marsala and Mazara del Vallo; and from Messina to Syracuse via Catania. Services within other areas are slow or require a change (there is no direct train from Palermo to Catania, for example). Almost everywhere else is best reached by bus (see below). For this reason, none of the usual European rail passes represent good value in Sicily, unless the island is just one stage of a longer Italian or European trip.

There are several different train services, of which the most common are the plush InterCity (IC) services and the more common regional trains (REG). (Sicily has no Eurostar Italia trains.) All can be booked at **trenitalia.com**, where the type of train is indicated with the initials IC or REG. 'Amica' fares are cheaper advance tickets (if you can find one); flexi-fare costs more but is flexible; and standard fare is just that. Booking and buying tickets at the counter or via machines in train stations is convenient if you can't access the internet. Tickets must be validated at the yellow stamping machines before boarding.

Sicily also has a private train line, called the **Circumetnea**, which circles the base of Mount Etna.

Road

Car Driving in Sicily is not for the timid. Sicilians drive with reckless disregard for road markings, traffic lights, and pedestrians. Don't hesitate (or you will be lost) and remember that the golden rule of Sicilian driving is to keep the traffic flowing.

Italy has strict laws on drink driving: the legal limit is 0.5 g of alcohol per litre of blood (roughly one glass of wine or beer), so steer clear of alcohol to be safe. The use of mobile telephones while driving is illegal. Children under 1.5 m are required to sit in the back of the car, and a reflective jacket must be worn if your car breaks down on the carriageway in poor visibility. On-the-spot fines for minor traffic offences are now legal – typically €150-250. Always get a receipt if you incur one.

Speed limits are 130 kph (motorways), 110 kph (dual carriageways) and 50 kph (towns). Limits are 20 kph *lower* on motorways and dual carriageways when the road is wet. *Autostrade* (motorways) are toll roads, so keep cash in the car as a back-up even though you can use credit cards on the blue 'viacard' gates. **Autostrade** ⓘ *T0840-042121 for road conditions, autostrade.it*, provides information on motorways in Italy, while **Automobile Club d'Italia (ACI)** ⓘ *T803116, aci.it*, provides general driving information. ACI offers roadside assistance with English-speaking operators. Unleaded petrol is *benzina*, diesel is *gasolio*.

Car hire Car hire is available at all of Italy's international airports and many domestic airports. Book as early as possible for popular destinations and at busy times of year. Check in advance the opening times of the car hire office. Car hire comparison websites and agents are a good place to start a search for the best deals. Try **easycar.com**, **carrentals.co.uk**, **thinksicily.com** (which has a good price comparison engine).

Check what documents are required. Some companies will ask for an International Driving Licence, with your normal driving licence, if the language of your driving licence is different from the country you're renting the car in. Others are content with an EU licence. You'll need to produce a credit card for most companies. If you book ahead, make sure that the credit card holder is the same as the person renting and driving the car to avoid any problems. Most companies have a lower age limit of 21 years and require that you've held your licence for at least a year. Many have a young driver surcharge for those under 25. Confirm insurance and any damage waiver charges and keep all your documents with you when you drive. Always take a printed copy of the contract with you, regardless of whether you have a booking number and a 'confirmed' booking.

Bicycle Cycling is madness in Sicilian cities and in general the island is poorly equipped for cyclists. Bike rental outlets are few and far between, even in the biggest resorts, and there are almost no cycling lanes anywhere. However, there are some superb cycling routes for experienced road cyclists, particularly in the Madonie mountains and around Mount Etna, and some flatter routes, more suitable for less experienced bikers, in the west. These are popular with foreign visitors, most of whom bring their own bikes or come on organized holidays.

Bus/coach Buses are the most popular – and often the only – means of public transport in Sicily. There are four main bus companies which cover most of the island: **AST** (aziendasicilianatrasporti.it); **SAIS** (saisautolinee.it); **Interbus** (interbus.it); and **Giuntabus** (giuntabus.com). These are supplemented by numerous local bus services. Tickets can usually be bought on board, or at kiosks near bus stops or bus stations in larger towns. Tickets for city buses should be purchased before boarding and must be validated once you get on (or risk a fine). Tickets are generally purchased at ticket booths, tobacco shops (*tabacchi*), or newspaper kiosks.

Sea
Ferry and hydrofoil Sicily's offshore islands are linked by ferry and hydrofoil. Porto Empedocle is the main port for for the Pelagie Islands. The main ferry lines are operated by **Ustica** (usticalines.it) and **Siremar** (siremar.it).

Where to stay in Palermo and the Northwest

Whether you want to hobnob with the stars in a *palazzo* in Taormina, or help out with the olive harvest on a country estate, you'll be spoilt for choice in Sicily, which offers a wide range of accommodation for all tastes and pockets. Not so long ago, the pickings weren't so rich, but recent years have seen the rise of the boutique hotel, the quirky B&B, and the stylish *agriturismo*. Unfortunately, these options are largely confined to the cities, coastal resorts and major tourist attractions: as soon as you head off the beaten track, the options become more limited. Many towns and villages of the interior have no accommodation at all, although, if they like the look of you, staff in the tourist offices may be able to put you in touch with someone offering *camere* (rooms). If you are travelling with your own transport, *agriturismi* are often the best rural options, but anyone travelling by public transport should plan acccommodation carefully in advance.

Prices soar in the high season, particularly on the islands and along the coast. For four weeks in late July and August, expect everything to cost three or four times what it would a month later, and plan accordingly. Affordable accommodation is often booked solid for this period, so reserve quickly. Many hotels require full or half board during the peak season, and it's wise to check before you book. Note that many of the island hotels close over the winter months.

Useful websites

Villas and apartments
discoversicily.com.
opensicily.com
ownersdirect.co.uk
perfectplaces.com
solosicily.com
thinksicily.com

Agriturismi
agriturismo.com.
agriturismosicilia.it
agriturist.it
siciliariturismo.com (Italian only)
toprural.com

Hotels
destinia.com
hotels.com
travelnow.com.
venere.com

B&Bs
bbplanet.it
bedandbreakfast.com
bed-and-breakfast-sicilia.it

Hostels and *rifugi*
ostellionline.org
bug.co.uk
hostelbookers.com
realadventures.com

Villas and apartments
Self-catering is often a good idea if you are travelling with the family or in a large group. Sicily offers a range of splendid seaside villas (one tour company offers a particularly luxurious option which is voted 'best villa in the Mediterranean' year after year), with most concentrated around the tourist mecca of Taormina. Self-catering apartments by the sea are very popular with the Italians, particularly on the islands, and you'll be hard pressed to find any available in August unless you book well in advance. These are usually much cheaper than hotels, although they are often basic and located in the standard concrete holiday blocks that are a feature of every Italian seaside resort. Increasingly, *agriturismi* are offering self-catering accommodation, often in attractively converted stables or outhouses. See also box above – thinksicily.com and opensicily.com are both highly recommended.

Agriturismi
Perhaps the best way to visit Sicily is to stay on one of the island's superb *agriturismi* (farm accommodation). There is a huge range available, from palatial accommodation with pool and restaurant (to rival any luxury hotel) to simple farms with rustic rooms. Farm holidays have become increasingly popular throughout Italy over the last few years, particularly with families, and some offer plenty of child-friendly extras such as play areas and children's pools. Most are on working farms, and some allow guests to take part in the harvest, or prepare meals with produce grown on the estate. Others include specific activities, such as horse riding or tours of Mount Etna. A new initiative has seen the lands confiscated from Mafia leaders being transformed into working farms with accommodation: the idea behind the scheme is to provide much-needed work for locals so that they can resist joining the Mafia through poverty. See also Useful websites, above.

Hotels
The swankiest hotels are clustered in Taormina, followed by the main cities and resorts. Four- or five-star accommodation is virtually unheard of in Sicily's interior, although some

Price codes

Where to stay
€€€€ over €300   €€€ €200-300
€€ €100-200   € under €100
Prices refer to the cost of two people sharing a double room in the high season.

Restaurants
€€€€ over €40   €€€ €30-40
€€ €20-30   € under €20
Prices refer to the average cost of a two-course meal for one person, including drinks and service charge.

---

agriturismi offer luxurious hotel-style services. The craze for boutique hotels that has swept the rest of the world in the last decade has been slow to reach Sicily but, finally, the word is out and the island can now offer some sumptuous designer accommodation. There is still plenty of dreary, chain-hotel-style accommodation, so popular in the 1970s and 1980s, but the classic peeling *palazzo* with creaking furniture and a rosary on the wall has almost had its day.

There are scores of hotel-booking websites. These tend to concentrate on mainstream hotels and the more expensive ones. Note that the star rating refers to services rather than difficult-to-rate features such as charm or service. This can lead to anomalies such as a stunning little hotel with rooms filled with antiques but no lift earning a lower rating than a concrete monstrosity with a cafeteria and as much soul as an airport waiting lounge. Star ratings are also rarely an indication of price, particularly on the islands, where some of the most expensive hotels on Sicily have only a two- or three-star rating.

B&Bs

The biggest recent change in the Sicilian accommodation scene has been the proliferation of B&Bs. These vary wildly, from a simple room in a converted *palazzo* to private homes full of chintzy flounces. Many of the smaller towns without hotel accommodation will have a few B&Bs. Tourist information offices can usually provide details. Like hotels, there has been a definite swing towards the cool and stylish in recent years. Prices are usually very reasonable, and B&Bs will usually offer better accommodation than hotels for the same price.

Hostels and rifugi

There are only five official youth hostels on Sicily. These can be found in the major tourist centres Palermo, Catania, Piazza Armerina and Noto, and in the rural town of Castroreale. Siracusa, Taormina and the Aeolian Islands offer independently run backpacker accommodation. Prices start at around €18 for a dorm bed. Only official youth hostels (aighostels.com, including online reservations) require membership of a hostelling organization. For suggestions on independent backpacker hostels, check out Useful websites, opposite.

For walkers and climbers, Italy's system of *rifugi* (mountain huts) offer basic (usually extremely basic) accommodation in rural mountainous areas: in Sicily they can be found in the Madonie and Nebrodi ranges, and also on Mount Etna. The *rifugi* are run by the **Club**

Alpino Italiano (cai.it, some sections of the website are exclusively in Italian) and are open to non-members. Advance booking is essential.

Convents and monasteries

Several convents and monasteries offer simple accommodation to visitors. These are rarely advertised and it can be hard to find information, but the Italian tourist office can provide lists in advance of your trip. An easier way of arranging a monastery stay may be to contact a specialist tour operator, such as **Monastery Stays** (monasterystays.com), which can arrange rooms at twelve properties throughout the island (prices range from €44 to €188 for a double room, which includes the booking fee).

Food and drink in Palermo and the Northwest

Even in a country famed for its passion for food, the Sicilians stand out. Andrea Camilleri's hugely popular fictional detective and gourmand, Inspector Montalbano, can be silenced by a perfectly prepared dish of *caponata*, and spends at least as much time pondering what to eat and where to eat it as he does capturing criminals.

Sicilian cuisine

The island's cuisine is wonderfully rich, combining the wide range of local ingredients with an infusion of flavours bequeathed by Greeks, Normans, Spanish and, perhaps most pervasively, Arabs and, later, North Africans. It's not surprising that the Slow Food Movement (founded in Italy in the 1980s as a protest against 'fast food') flourishes in Sicily; few cuisines place such emphasis on the importance of fresh, seasonal produce, or so carefully cherish their traditional foods.

Every town and village has its street market, with stalls piled high with seasonal produce: zingy blood oranges and citrus fruit in winter, mounds of artichokes and broad beans in spring, then melons and peaches, and the bursting figs and *fichi d'india* (prickly pear) of late summer, and then the pungent mushrooms of autumn. By the side of every road is a three-wheeled truck (known as *ape*, meaning bee) overflowing with whatever is in season. And even if you don't speak a word of Italian, you can bet your last euro that the impassioned exchange between the stallholder and the client has something to do with food.

The cuisine follows the landscape, as well as the seasons. On the coast, fish predominates, particularly swordfish and tuna, although octopus, squid and a dazzling range of shellfish is also available. In some of the smaller coastal towns, you can head to the quay to buy the catch of the day directly from the fishermen. A visit to Catania's celebrated fish market is one of the best experiences to be had on the island. Inland, meat features more prominently on the menu, particularly pork and lamb, which is often served simply grilled, barbecue-style, over hot coals. The inland regions, particularly the Madonie and Nebrodi mountains, also enjoy a superb reputation for artisanal cheeses, including *provola*, *ragusano* and *caciocavallo*, and all kinds of hams and cured sausages. Black Nebrodi pigs, which live semi-wild in the forest, are the source of highly regarded *prosciutto* and other pork products.

Great, universally known Sicilian dishes include: *pasta alla Norma*, named apparently after Bellini's opera, and prepared with aubergine, tomatoes and a pungent, cured ricotta cheese; *caponata*, a sort of ratatouille made with aubergine, peppers and tomatoes; *cuscus al pesce*, North African-style couscous served with fish rather than meat; and *pasta con le sarde*, which is made with sardines, anchovies and fennel.

Sicily is also famous for its snack foods, including *arancine*, stuffed, fried rice balls which usually contain a filling made with minced meat, peas, tomato sauce, and mozzarella, although there are many variations.

Desserts and pastries

Sicilians are famous the world over for their outstanding sweet pastries. Top desserts include *cannolli*, pastry tubes filled with a creamy, sweet ricotta filling, and *cassata*, a rich cake stuffed with more creamy ricotta, but every town and village has its own particular speciality and a visit to the *pasticceria* is always a treat. The ice cream (*gelati*) is outstanding, and often freshly prepared with whichever fruit is in season; try it local style, served inside a soft brioche roll.

When and where to eat

Colazione (breakfast) in Sicily usually consists of a *caffè latte* or an *espresso* accompanied by a pastry, usually a croissant-shaped cornetto with fillings – *alla crema* (pastry cream), *al cioccolato* (chocolate) or *alla marmellata* (marmalade). At weekends, particularly on Sundays, Sicilians will enjoy a long *pranzo* (lunch), which will inevitably be followed by a siesta in the deadening heat of summer. In the evenings, after the *passeggiata*, locals might head to a café terrace for an *aperitivo*.

Although traditionally *ristoranti* were a cut above less formal *trattorie*, this distinction has now been blurred to the point at which it is no longer any indication of the quality of an establishment. *Ristorante-pizzerie* serve pizzas (which are almost as good as those in Naples), but will often also offer a wide range of local meat, fish and pasta dishes. A full lunch or dinner Italian-style usually begins with *antipasti*, often a selection of cold dishes at a self-service buffet. For the first course, *il primo*, it's usual to have a pasta dish or perhaps some soup. *Il secondo* is the meat or fish dish, which will probably be served unaccompanied, so you will probably have to order vegetable *contorni* (side dishes). Curiously, in a region famed for its sweet delicacies, restaurant *dolci* (desserts) are rarely good, and it's best to stick to fresh fruit (and head to the nearest *pasticceria* after the meal) unless you know the desserts are home-made.

Restaurants usually serve lunch from 1200 to 1530 and dinner from 1900 to 2300. If you get the munchies between meals, look for a *távola calda* ('hot table'). These simple snack bars sell all the delicious Sicilian fast foods, from *arancine* to mini-pizzas.

Wines of Sicily

Sicily is one of Italy's largest wine-producing areas, and local wine, once a byword for cheap plonk, has become increasingly sophisticated in recent years, with a full spectrum of wines being made from both indigenous (such as Nero d'Avola, Catarrato and Grillo) and international grape varieties. There are several regional liqueurs, made from almonds, or prickly pear, and Sicilian *limoncello* is deliciously zesty.

Few of the DOC (*Denominazione di Origine Controllata*) areas are well known outside the island – the most prominent wine regions are Etna in the east, Alcamo in the northwest in Trapani province, and Marsala in the west.

Alcamo Perhaps best known for its dry yet fruity Bianco di Alcamo, the perfect accompaniment to seafood. Produced southwest of Palermo.
Cerasuolo di Vittoria A pale-coloured yet full-bodied, dry red with aromas of cherries from the Ragusa region.

Etna Currently the hottest wine-producing area with a range of reds, rosés and whites from fashionable new wineries, including one belonging to Mick Hucknall of Simply Red.
Faro A popular, medium-bodied red grown in the Messina region.
Malvasia delle Lipari This is a stunning sweet wine produced in the Aeolian Islands, particularly on Lipari.
Marsala Sicily's most famous tipple, the key ingredient in that most popular of Italian desserts, *zabaglione*. An Italian equivalent to sherry and port, this fortified wine was popularized by the British in the early 19th century. It comes in a variety of forms including dry, medium or sweet, and is available as *oro* (golden), *ambra* (amber) and *rubino* (ruby). It is most commonly drunk as an aperitif, or to accompany dessert.
Moscato Sweet dessert wines are made in Siracusa and Noto, but the most celebrated wines come from Pantelleria, where sweet wines of varying styles – *passito* (from dried grapes) and *non-passito*, some fortified, some sparkling – are made from the Zibibbo (Muscat of Alexandria) grape, much as they were five hundred years ago.

Some of the most famous wine producers include Regaleali, which spearheaded the revival of Sicilian wines and is still probably the most popular producer on the island, as well as Rallo (Donnafugata), Planeta (Noto), Pellegrino (Marsala), Moncada Rudini (Pachino) and Murgo (Etna).

Festivals in Palermo and the Northwest

January
Festa Nazionale della Befana (6th)
Epiphany, which marks the end of the Christmas celebrations, is traditionally the day on which Italian children are given presents. An old witch, Befana, who refused to accompany the Magi to find Jesus in the stable, rewards good children with sweets, and bad children with a lump of coal. There are special masses and celebrations throughout the island, and each town prepares its own bread and cakes.
Arbëresh (6th) The feast of the Epiphany (12 days after Christmas) is celebrated in Piana degli Albanesi according to ancient rites and traditions passed down from the first Albanian immigrants who arrived here in the 15th century. Exquisite embroidered Balkan costumes, made by hand, are worn in elaborate processions and religious rites. The highlight is a solemn re-enactment of the Baptism of Christ.

February
Festa del Mandorlo (first week) This festival celebrating the almond blossom in Agrigento, where thousands of almond trees fill the Valle dei Templi with their pale pink blooms. There are puppet shows, music, parades and street parties, and bakeries and street stalls sell all kinds of delicious almond treats.
Carnevale (10 days before Ash Wednesday) *carnevaledisciacca.it*. Carnival is celebrated across the island, but one of the best events is famously held in Sciacca. Townspeople spend the entire year decorating the floats with vast historical, mythical or allegorical scenes made of papier-mâché, many of which feature popular TV personalities, celebrities or politicians. Each neighbourhood vies to produce the winning float. The anarchic figure of Peppe 'Nnappa begins the carnival celebrations by dancing through the streets and inviting the crowds to join

in. He leads another fabulous procession of elaborate floats, often hilarious spoofs of contemporary scandals. The floats are created by neighbourhood collectives, who vie with each other to build the best float.

March/April
Pasqua (Easter) *La Settima Santa* (Easter week) is celebrated with solemn processions throughout the island, with each town or village preparing special cakes and breads according to time-honoured recipes. The most famous Easter celebrations take place in Trapani, where the *Processione dei Misteri* – the procession of enormous floats bearing sculptural depictions of the Passion of Christ by members of different trade guilds – lasts from 1400 on Good Friday to 1200 on Saturday.

In the mountain town of Gangi, there is an unusual competition between supporters of the Madonna and supporters of Jesus, who vie to produce the most beautiful decorations on the cathedral square on Easter Sunday.

In Piano degli Albanesi, Easter celebrations follow Greek Orthodox traditions and begin with the arrival of the archbishop on horseback on Palm Sunday. There are processions, choirs sing sacred songs, and full-immersion baptisms are performed by white-robed priests. On Easter Sunday, the festival culminates with Mass in the cathedral of San Demetrio followed by a huge feast.

In Terrasini, near Palermo, the Festa degli Schietti (Batchelors' Festival) is celebrated on Easter Sunday. Batchelors lift a beautifully decorated orange tree with just one hand to show their strength to their fiancées.

Prizzi also has its own unusual tradition, the *Aballu de li Diavoli* (Dance of the Devils), which dates back to medieval times and culminates in a horde of 'devils' in masks rampaging through the town.

June
Palermo Estate and Verdura Festival (June to September) The Palermo Summer Festival takes place from June to September, with a varied programme of events including street theatre, concerts and puppet shows. The Teatro Massimo runs a varied programme of opera, pop, flamenco, jazz and theatre during the summer months. Ask the tourist office for information.

July
Festino di Santa Rosalia (9-15th) The festival in honour of Palermo's patron saint, Santa Rosalia, is one of the biggest and most popular traditional events in Sicily. The saint is believed to have saved the city from plague in 1624, and her feast is celebrated with processions, concerts, street theatre and fireworks.

September
Il Pellegrinaggio alla Madonna del Tindari (8th) The Black Madonna of Tindari is one of the most venerated statues in Sicily, and thousands join the annual pilgrimage to the sanctuary, which begins on the night of the 7th. On the 8th, there is a Mass with choirs from across the island, a lively street fair and a huge fireworks show.

Couscous Fest (22nd-27th) *San Vito Lo Capo, sanvitocouscous.com*. The famous Sicilian dish of couscous with fish, a fusion of North African and Mediterranean influences, is the focus of a huge, popular festival in San Vito Lo Capo, where there are tastings, concerts and street parties.

October
Festa di Maria SS del Lume (14th) *Santa Flavia*. One of the most picturesque local festivals takes place in Santa Flavia, in honour of the Madonna of the Holiest of Light. A procession of fishing boats, lit with torches, is followed by the blessing of the statue, which is submerged in the port.

November
Tutti i Santi (All Saints' Day) (1st) All Saints' Day is a national holiday celebrated across Sicily. This is the Italian version of Halloween (which is increasingly celebrated), when children often dress up in frightening costumes, and *pasticceries* are full of traditional confectionery. The following day, the Day of the Dead, children traditionally hunt for sweets and toys left overnight by the 'souls of the dead', and families take picnics and visit their relatives' graves, decorating them with candles and flowers.

December
Presepi di Natale One of the most unusual features of the Christmas period in Italy, including Sicily, are the 'living' nativity scenes, or *presepi viventi*, which take place in several towns. Costumed townspeople re-enact the arrival of the Magi. Manger scenes can be found in most towns.

Essentials A-Z

Customs and immigration
UK and EU citizens do not need a visa, but will need a valid passport to enter Italy. A standard tourist visa for those from outside the EU is valid for up to 90 days.

Disabled travellers
Italy is rather behind when it comes to catering for disabled travellers, and Sicily, which is one of the poorest regions in Italy, is worse than almost anywhere else. There is an interesting and inspiring article describing a trip to Sicily by a pair of independent wheelchair-users at globalaccessnews.com/sicilyedwards08.htm. Before departure, contact a specialist association or agency for more details, such as **Accessible Italy** (accessibleitaly.com) or **Society for Accessible Travel and Hospitality** (sath.org).

Emergency numbers
Ambulance T118; **Fire** T115; **Police** T112 (with English-speaking operators), T113 (*carabinieri*); Roadside assistance T803116.

Etiquette
Projecting a good image is important to Sicilians. Smart casual dress is expected, even in summer when other countries dress down. At clubs and fashionable restaurants in the cities and resorts, you'll need to dress up to get in. Take note of public notices about conduct: sitting on steps or eating and drinking in certain historic areas is not allowed. Covering arms and legs is necessary for admission into some churches. Punctuality is apparently not mandatory in Italy, so be prepared to wait – even at government-run sights where opening times are treated as a suggestion.

Families
Whether for a traditional beach break or an afternoon in a *gelateria*, families are well accommodated in Italy. The family is highly regarded in Italy and *bambini* are indulged and there's plenty to do for children besides endless museum visits. Do note that sometimes lone parents or adults accompanying children of a different surname may need evidence before taking children in and out of the country. Contact your Italian embassy for current details: in London T020-7312 2200, in Washington DC T202-518-2139, in Dublin T353-1-660-1744, in Ottawa T613-232-2401, in Canberra T612-6273-3333.

Health
Comprehensive travel and medical insurance is strongly recommended for all travel. EU citizens should apply for a free **European Health Insurance Card** (ehic.org) which replaced the E111 form and offers reduced-cost medical treatment.

Pharmacies are identified by a large green cross outside. The **Farmacie di Turno** (duty pharmacies, which take it in turn to open 24 hours) are listed on the front door. Call T1100 for addresses of the nearest open pharmacies. The accident and emergency department of a hospital is called the *pronto soccorso*. Local hospital details are listed in the Directory sections for each destination.

Insurance
Comprehensive travel and medical insurance is strongly recommended for all travel – the EHIC is not a replacement for insurance. You should check any exclusions, and that your policy covers you for all the activities you want to undertake. Keep details of your insurance documents separately – emailing yourself with the details is a good way to keep the information safe and accessible. Ensure you have full insurance if hiring a car, and you might need an international insurance certificate if taking your own car (contact your current insurers).

Money

The Italian currency is the Euro (€). Throughout Sicily there are ATMs that accept major credit and debit cards. To change cash or travellers' cheques, look for a *cambio*. Most larger restaurants and shops take major credit cards, but smaller establishments, museums and art galleries rarely accept them. Sicily is still a cash-based society. Paying directly with debit cards such as Cirrus is almost impossible, so withdrawing from an ATM and paying cash is better. Keep plenty of cash for toll roads if you're driving.

You could scrape by on €45-60 per person per day if you stay at hostels and cater for yourself. For a modest budget holiday, allow around €90-100 each for food, accommodation and travel. For double this sum, you can live in absolute comfort. Prices are considerably higher on the coast and on the islands, particularly during the intense main season (end-July to end-August) when accommodation prices can double or even triple. The good things in life are still cheap: a scoop of the best ice cream you'll ever taste is as little as €1.20. Stand at the bar for your breakfast *cornetto e cappuccino* and you'll only have to fork out about €1.80-2.00 (double that to sit on a gorgeous, but touristy square).

Opening hours and holidays

Opening hours vary widely across the island, but the following is a very general guide. Shops and businesses are usually open from Monday to Saturday 0900-1300 and then from around 1530-1930. Everywhere is closed on Sunday, apart from bakeries and cake shops. Businesses often close completely for the whole of August. Restaurants usually open at lunchtimes around 1230 and close around 1500, opening again at 1900 until about 2200 or 2300. Pizzerias may not open at lunchtimes, and, if they do, they probably won't serve pizza (this is because it takes such a long time to get the wood-fired ovens going).

Museums are usually open during the mornings only (0900-1300) in smaller towns, with afternoon opening just one or two days a week. They are often closed on Sunday afternoons and sometimes on Mondays. The main archaeological sites are usually open from 0900 to one hour before dusk.

Note that opening times in Sicily are, at best, guidelines. Even the biggest and most important sights can close without warning. If there is something you really want to see, ring in advance to ensure it is open – and always, always have a plan B.

Police

While it appears that there are several different types of police in Italy (and several uniforms for each), there are two you will see most often: the *polizia* (T113) and the *carabinieri* (T112). The *polizia* are the 'normal' police under the control of the Interior Ministry, while the *carabinieri* are a de facto military force. Both will respond if you need help.

Post

Italian post has a not entirely undeserved reputation for being unreliable, particularly for handling postcards. Overseas post will require *posta prioritaria* (priority mail) and a postcard stamp will cost from €0.65. You can buy *francobolli* (stamps) at post offices and *tabacchi* (look for T signs).

Safety

The crime rate in Italy is generally low, but rates of petty crime higher. Take general care when travelling: don't flaunt your valuables, take only what money you need and split it, and don't take risks you wouldn't at home. Beware of scams and con artists, and don't expect things to go smoothly if you partake in fake goods. Car break-ins are common, so always remove valuables and open the glove compartment to show that there is nothing valuable inside the car. Take care on public transport where pickpockets or bag-cutters might operate. Do not make it clear which stop you're getting off at – it gives potential thieves a timeframe to work in (most work in groups). Female travellers will find Sicily quite safe, apart from some attention from local Lotharios, who are generally harmless.

Telephone
The dialing codes for the main towns in the region are: Palermo 091; Messina 090; Catania 095; Syracuse 093; Agrigento 0922; Trapani 0923; Enna 0935. You need to use these local codes even when dialling from within the city or region. The prefix for Italy is +39. You no longer need to drop the initial '0' from area codes when calling from abroad. For directory enquiries call T12.

Time difference
Italy uses Central European Time, GMT+1.

Tipping
Most waiters in the region expect a tip from foreigners; 10-15% is the norm if you're really happy with the service. Leaving change from the bill is appropriate for cheaper *enotecas* and osterias. Taxis may add on extra costs for luggage etc but an additional tip is always appreciated. Rounding up prices always goes down well, especially if it means avoiding having to give change – not a favourite Italian habit.

Tourist information
Tourist information in Sicily is patchy at best. While a few tourist information offices are well equipped and have multilingual staff on hand to help, most have nothing but the unfailing charm of the attendants. A basic overview of Sicily is provided by the Italian tourist board at italia.it, while the official Sicilian tourism website regione.sicilia.it/turismo is a sometimes outdated but occasionally useful source of information before you travel. There are local tourist information offices in most towns, run by several different bodies, and with a confusing array of acronyms. If you ask simply for the 'ufficio turistico', you will be sent in the right direction. In smaller towns, the municipally run local tourist offices are called Pro Loco. The larger towns may have regional tourist offices – Ente Provinciale per il Turismo (EPT) or Azienda di Promozione Turistica (APT) – which provide information on the province. In big cities, like Catania and Palermo, there are also information offices run by Informazioni e Assistenza ai Turisti (IAT) or Azienda Autonoma de di Soggiorno e Turismo (AAST).

Admission fees
There are no useful discount passes in Sicily. Reduced admission fees are usually available to children, students, and seniors. Some museums offer free admission to EU citizens on production of a passport. Museums are, however, generally inexpensive.

Voltage
Italy functions on a 220V mains supply and the standard European two-pin plug.

Contents

24 Palermo
- 25 Palazzo dei Normanni and around
- 26 *Map: Palermo*
- 28 Corso Vittorio Emanuele and Quattro Canti
- 30 La Kalsa
- 32 Around La Vucciria
- 33 Il Capo
- 34 Around via Libertà
- 34 Palermo fringes
- 36 Listings

41 Around Palermo
- 42 North of Palermo
- 42 South of Palermo
- 43 Coast towards Cefalù
- 45 Cefalù
- 47 Around Cefalù
- 47 Ustica
- 49 Listings

Footprint features

31 A walking tour through La Kalsa

Palermo & around

Palermo

When the 12th-century traveller Ibn Jubayr first saw Palermo, sprawled around a vast bay, he exclaimed "it dazzles the eyes with its perfection". A thousand years have taken their toll, but the 20th century came close to sounding the city's death knell: wartime destruction was followed by postwar desecration, as corrupt officials tried to rip out its ancient heart. Crushing poverty and the stranglehold of the Mafia almost wiped out what was left. But modern Palermo is experiencing an extraordinary revival. Bomb-blasted ruins are now exciting cultural centres and galleries. Parts of the historic centre are being transformed from no-go areas to places to see and be seen, and the famous markets assault every sense with their noise and colour. Palermo may still be poor and chaotic, but it's also utterly intoxicating – and, for the first time in decades, optimistic.

Palazzo dei Normanni and around → *For listings, see pages 36-40.*

The Palazzo dei Normanni (Norman Palace), now seat of the Sicilian parliament, contains the ravishing Cappella Palatina, a jewel of Romanesque art. The palace is flanked on one side by the cathedral and a line of splendid *palazzi* along corso Vittorio Emanuele. On the other is the Albergheria, one of Palermo's poorest yet most historic districts, with a colourful market.

Palazzo dei Normanni and Cappella Palatina
ⓘ *Piazza Indipendenza, T091-705 6001, ars.sicilia.it. Mon-Fri 0900-1200, 1400-1700 (last entry 1630), Sun and holidays 0830-1400, Fri-Sun €8.50/6.50 18-25s, Tue-Thu €7/5 18-25s, free under 18 and over 65. May close without warning for official functions.*

Phoenicians and Romans built a fortress on this gentle incline, but the Arabs were the first to build a palace, after they moved the Sicilian capital to Palermo from Syracuse in the ninth century. The Normans remodelled and enlarged it considerably in the 12th and 13th centuries, and the Spanish added the grand façade in the 1600s. The main reason to visit is the stunning Cappella Palatina, with its wealth of Byzantine mosaics. In order to see the exquisite little Sala di Re Ruggero upstairs, you will have to submit to the otherwise dull tour of the palace's 19th-century Royal Apartments.

The **Cappella Palatina** is a royal chapel, built for Roger II in the mid-12th century by the finest mosaic artists, sculptors and wood-carvers of the age. The differing styles and techniques – Greek, Byzantine, Arabic and Norman – are perfectly synthesized in this chapel, considered the apogee of the Sicilian Romanesque style. The chapel may be tiny, but it is so thoroughly enthralling that you could easily spend a couple of hours here (even though some sections are under scaffolding as part of an ongoing restoration project). Look up to see the superb ceiling, intricately carved, and down to see the inlaid marble floor. The walls, columns and domes are entirely filled with mosaic decoration, with stories from the Bible unfolding magically across the breadth of the chapel.

Upstairs, a guided tour of the **Royal Apartments** takes you through a series of dull 19th-century salons awhirl with velvet and gilt before arriving at the other great jewel of the palace: the **Sala di Re Ruggero** (Salon of King Roger), filled with exotic mosaics depicting peacocks and palm trees, all delicately picked out in glowing colours.

Albergheria
The Albergheria – defined roughly by via Maqueda, corso Tukory and corso Vittorio Emanuele – is one of the city's oldest and poorest districts, still badly scarred by bomb damage from the Second World War. Many of the surviving tenements are tenuously propped up with rusty supports, and the poverty is tangible. However, it's deeply atmospheric, not least thanks to the presence of the 1000-year-old street market, the **Mercato di Ballarò**, located on and around piazza Ballarò. There are a couple of handsome churches, including **Chiesa del Gesù** ⓘ *Mon-Sat 0800-1130, 1700-1830, Sun and holidays 0800-1230*, the first Jesuit church in Sicily. The multi-coloured, tiled dome of the **Chiesa di Santa Maria del Carmine** ⓘ *daily 0830-1230*, rises above the rooftops on the piazza del Carmine and contains more splendid Baroque decoration, including stucco work by Giacomo Serpotta. Just off the Piazza Ballarò is the **Chiesa di San Nicolò all'Albergheria** ⓘ *via Nunzio Nasi 18, T0916 512820, open only for mass Mon-Sat at 1730, Sun 1030 and 1600*, which dates back to the 13th century but was fussily remodelled in the 16th and 17th

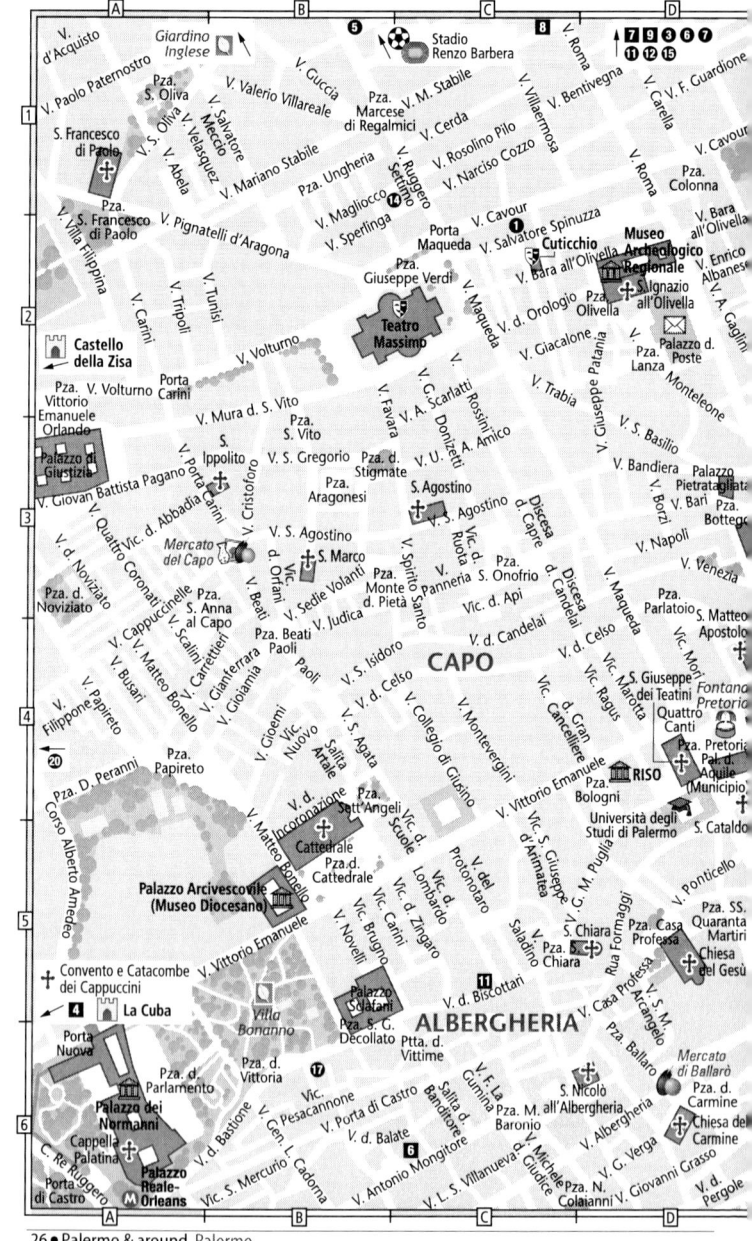

26 • Palermo & around Palermo

Where to stay

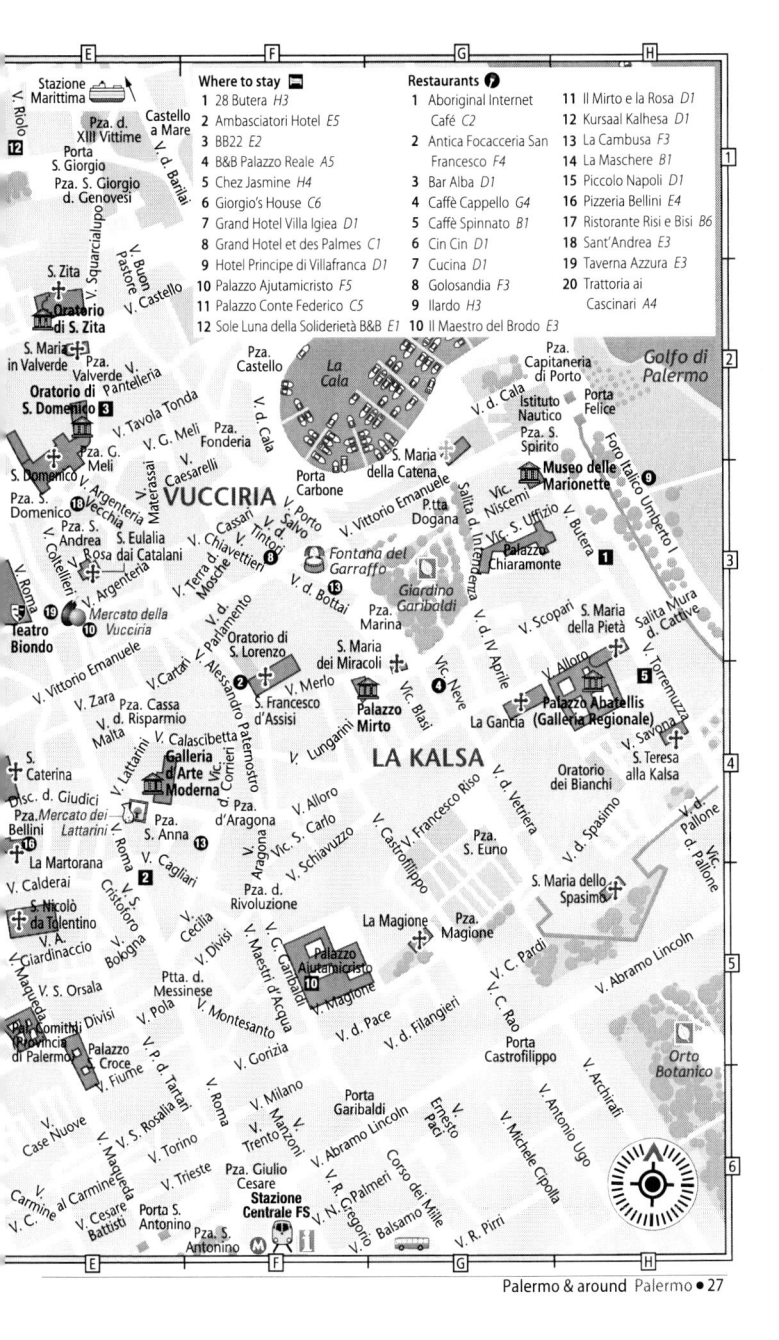

1 28 Butera *H3*
2 Ambasciatori Hotel *E5*
3 BB22 *E2*
4 B&B Palazzo Reale *A5*
5 Chez Jasmine *H4*
6 Giorgio's House *C6*
7 Grand Hotel Villa Igiea *D1*
8 Grand Hotel et des Palmes *C1*
9 Hotel Principe di Villafranca *D1*
10 Palazzo Ajutamicristo *F5*
11 Palazzo Conte Federico *C5*
12 Sole Luna della Solidarietà B&B *E1*

Restaurants

1 Aboriginal Internet Café *C2*
2 Antica Focacceria San Francesco *F4*
3 Bar Alba *D1*
4 Caffè Cappello *G4*
5 Caffè Spinnato *B1*
6 Cin Cin *D1*
7 Cucina *D1*
8 Golosandia *F3*
9 Ilardo *H3*
10 Il Maestro del Brodo *E3*
11 Il Mirto e la Rosa *D1*
12 Kursaal Kalhesa *D1*
13 La Cambusa *F3*
14 La Maschere *B1*
15 Piccolo Napoli *D1*
16 Pizzeria Bellini *E4*
17 Ristorante Risi e Bisi *B6*
18 Sant'Andrea *E3*
19 Taverna Azzura *E3*
20 Trattoria ai Cascinari *A4*

centuries. You can climb the belltower (opening hours are erratic, but €1.50) for wonderful views over the higgledy piggledy rooftops to the mountains in one direction and the sea in the other.

Cattedrale
ⓘ *Corso Vittorio Emanuele, T091-334373, cattedrale.palermo.it. Cathedral for worship Mon-Sat 0700-1900, Sun and holidays 0800-1300, 1600-1900. Tourist visits, treasury and crypt 0930-1730. Cathedral free, treasury and crypt €3/1 concession, €0.50 6 to 10, free under 6.*

On the other side of the royal palace, a short stroll down corso Vittorio Emanuele, looms Palermo's enormous cathedral. It was begun in the 12th century, when the ambitious Archbishop of Palermo, Gualtiero Offamiglio (an Englishman, whose name translates as Walter of the Mill), decided that a lavish cathedral to rival Monreale was the most effective way to trumpet the extent of his own power. Since then, the cathedral has acquired a hotch-potch of architectural styles, with a predominantly Catalan-Gothic exterior topped by an overblown 18th-century dome. The main entrance is a very beautiful early Gothic work, with three delicately sculpted arches, and superb 15th-century wooden doors.

The cavernous interior is a disappointment. A team of 18th-century meddlers stripped out what was left of its original decoration (the Norman mosaics had gone in the 1600s) and imposed their own bleak, Neoclassical vision. The only interesting side-chapel contains the reliquaries of Palermo's beloved Santa Rosalia, patroness of the city.

Medieval royal tombs are gathered at the back of the church. Roger II (1095-1154) is here, along with Frederick II (1194-1250) (see History, page 33) and his first wife Constance of Aragon (1179-1222). The pair were an odd couple: Constance was a 30-year-old widow when she married the 15-year-old king, but they were happy. Constance of Aragon's jewel-encrusted 13th-century crown takes pride of place in the Treasury, and there are more fine tombs in the crypt, including the mosaic-encrusted tomb of Walter of the Mill.

Museo Diocesano
ⓘ *Via Matteo Bonello 2, T091-607 7303, museodiocesanopa.it. Tue-Fri 0930-1330, Sat 1000-1800, Sun 0930-1330, €4.50/3 concession, €2 children under 6.*

The imposing Palazzo Arcivescovile (Archbishop's Palace), opposite the cathedral, houses a collection of religious art and sculpture, much of which was salvaged from ruins after the Second World War.

Palazzo Asmundo
ⓘ *Via Pietro Novelli 3, T091-651 9022, palazzoasmundo.it. Mon-Sat 0930-1300, hours may be extended for special exhibitions.*

Opposite the cathedral, this Baroque palace was begun in 1615 and enlarged by Giuseppe Asmundo Paternò, Marquis of Sessa, in the late 18th century. The opulent salons contains a superb collection of porcelain and *objets d'art*. It has a very pleasant little café for a break.

Corso Vittorio Emanuele and Quattro Canti

Linking the old port La Cala to the Palazzo dei Normanni, corso Vittorio Emanuele has been the city's main artery since Arabic times. No longer quite the grand address it once was, the corso is now blackened by traffic fumes, and amiable stray dogs sleep in the doorways of once-lavish *palazzi*.

Museo d'Arte Contemporanea della Sicilia
ⓘ *Palazzo Belmonte-Riso, corso Vittorio Emanuele 365, T091-320532, palazzoriso.it. Tue-Sun 1000-2000, Thu-Fri until 2200, €5, €3 students, free under 25 and over 60 with EU passports.*
A beautifully restored 18th-century *palazzo* makes a fabulous setting for one of Palermo's newest museums, dedicated to contemporary art and displaying paintings, photography and sculpture.

Quattro Canti
Halfway down corso Vittorio Emanuele, at the intersection with via Maqueda, Quattro Canti (Four Corners) marks the centre of the old city, the meeting point of its four historic districts. The grand Baroque *palazzi* at each corner of the junction are decorated with extravagant sculptures, each depicting one of the four seasons, a local saint, and various kings. Unfortunately, there's nowhere to get an overview, as the intersection is always choked with traffic.

Nearby, the impressive **piazza Pretoria** is named after the much-remodelled 15th-century Palazzo Pretorio (city hall), which overlooks a 16th-century Florentine fountain whose frolicking nymphs and satyrs so scandalized Palermitan society that they called it the **Fontana della Vergogna** (Fountain of Shame).

Piazza Bellini
ⓘ *Via Maqueda.*
Close to piazza Pretoria, piazza Bellini could be one of the very prettiest squares in Palermo if some enlightened city official would ban the traffic. The late 16th-century **Chiesa di Santa Caterina** belies its restrained exterior with a fabulously ornate Baroque interior, but is usually closed to visitors. Opposite, half-hidden by palm trees, sit two of Palermo's oldest and most beautiful churches: La Martorana and San Cataldo (see below). At the far end is the winsome **Teatro Bellini**, inaugurated in 1742, which still offers light opera.

Chiesa della Martorana
ⓘ *Piazza Bellini, T091-616 1692. Currently closed for restoration; enquire at the tourist office.*
Palermo's most celebrated medieval church, La Martorana, was founded in 1143 by George of Antioch, admiral to Roger II, and later given to a nearby convent endowed by Eloisa de Martorana. The nuns were responsible for the heavy-handed Baroque remodelling that took place in the 17th century, destroying the Norman apse and its irreplaceable mosaics, but fortunately they didn't demolish the delicate bell tower or strip the central cupola of its beautiful gilded depiction of Christ enthroned. These mosaics date back to the early 12th century and were probably carried out by artists from Constantinople. Other fragments of the original mosaics have been preserved near the entrance, including the only known portrait of Roger II in Sicily, which depicts him receiving his crown from Christ. The church is still used for Greek Orthodox services (held on Sunday mornings).

Chiesa di San Cataldo
ⓘ *Piazza Bellini, T091-616 1692. Apr-Oct Mon-Sat 0930-1300, 1530-1830, Nov-Mar daily 0930-1300, €2.50.*
Next to La Martorana, with its trio of small red domes peeping above the palm trees, San Cataldo was founded in the mid-12th century by Maio da Bari, hated advisor to William I. He died before its completion and so the interior was never finished; it remains almost completely bare, with just the mosaic floor to hint at its potential.

La Kalsa

Beyond piazza Bellini spreads the Kalsa district, one of the oldest neighbourhoods in Palermo. A thousand years ago, under the Arabs, it was a walled, exclusive district of palaces and gardens. Now it is poor and decrepit: ancient *palazzi* sag alarmingly, only the bombed-out shells of others survive. But the Kalsa is on the up, with new bars, clubs and galleries opening all the time.

Galleria di Arte Moderna e Restivo
ⓘ *Via Sant'Anna 21, T091-843 1605, galleriadartemodernapalermo.it. Tue-Sun 0930-1830, last entry 1730. €7/5 concession.*
Just off piazza Santa Anna, at the western end of via Alloro, the gallery of modern art contains paintings and sculpture from the 19th to the early 20th centuries, all beautifully laid out in light-filled galleries. It's a fashionable hang-out for arty young Sicilians, with a great café.

Galleria Regionale della Sicilia
ⓘ *Via Alloro 4, Palermo, T091-623 0061, regione.sicilia.it/beniculturali. Tue-Fri 0900-1800, Sat-Sun 0900-1300, €8/4 concession.*
The 15th-century Palazzo Abatellis contains the Galleria Regionale Siciliana, with the best collection of Sicilian painting and sculpture on the island. Among the highlights of the collection is the huge and terrifying fresco *The Triumph of Death*, by an unknown artist, in which Death careers wildly through a crowd on his skeletal steed. The finest work in the museum is Antonello da Messina's outstanding *Annunciation* (c1474), in which the Virgin is beautifully depicted trying to absorb the news which the angel has just imparted.

Piazza Marina and La Cala
The piazza Marina is a symbol of the Kalsa's regeneration: a decade or so ago, this square was squalid, dangerous and piled high with rubbish. Now it boasts good restaurants and a lovely public garden, the **Giardino di Garibaldi** (always open), where old-timers play dominoes under the banyan trees. One end of the square is dominated by the **Palazzo Chiaramonte** (occasionally open for exhibitions), once the seat of the Inquisition. At the opposite end, near via Merlo, is the 16th-century **Chiesa di Santa Maria dei Miracoli**. Behind the square is La Cala, the former port, now home to glossy yachts but still overlooked by the 15th-century Catalan-Gothic **Chiesa di Santa Maria della Catena** (open for mass).

Museo Internazionale delle Marionette Antonio Pasqualino
ⓘ *Piazzetta Niscemi 5 (just off piazza Marina), T091-328060, museomarionettepalermo.it. Mon-Fri 0900-1300, 1600-1830, Sat 0900-1300, €5/3 concession.*
There are more than 3000 puppets from around the world in this thoroughly enjoyable museum, which is run by a venerable family of puppeteers. Regular performances are held on Tuesday and Friday evenings from October to June.

Palazzo Mirto
ⓘ *Via Merlo 2, T091-616 4751. Tue-Fri 0900-1800, Sat-Sun 0900-1300, €4/2 concession. Combined ticket available (Galleria Regionale, Palazzo Mirto, Oratorio dei Bianchi) €10/5.*
Duck down the via Merlo, off piazza Marina, to find one of the few Palermitan *palazzi* open

A walking tour through La Kalsa

This walk takes you through one of Palermo's oldest and most interesting neighbourhoods, La Kalsa, where the ravages of time and neglect are slowly being reversed. The bomb damage of the Second World War is still evident, but now the blasted churches are used for concerts and festivals, and some Gothic *palazzi* accommodate boho-chic cafés and stylish restaurants. The walk culminates in beautiful public gardens.

Start at the **Quattro Canti** (see page 29) – where corso Vittorio Emanuele joins via Maqueda – which marks the intersection of Palermo's four historic quarters (*canti*). Of these, only the Albergheria (to the southwest) and the Kalsa (to the southeast) have survived. Walk down the via Maqueda, keeping the piazza Pretorio with its extravagant fountain on your left – aristocrats heading for the high-society church of San Giuseppe dei Teatini (on the right, opposite the square) were deeply offended by the fountain's ecstatic nymphs, and nuns from a nearby convent attacked it with sticks.

Turn left into the **piazza Bellini** (see page 29), where a pair of superb Norman churches, **La Martorana** (see page 29) and **San Cataldo** (see page 29), are framed by palm trees. Head towards the charming 18th-century **Teatro Bellini** and take the small street that skirts its left flank, the via Discesa di Guideca, which crosses via Roma and becomes **via Sant'Anna** by the Baroque church of the same name. You are now entering the Kalsa. Palermo's modern art gallery **Galleria di Arte Moderna e Restivo** (see page 30) is set in a restored former convent at via Sant'Anna 21, and contains a great café for a break. From the gallery, continue down via Sant'Anna, which soon becomes **via Alloro**, which is the Kalsa's main artery. Turn immediately right down **via Aragona**, which passes through the **piazza Rivoluzione** (so named because it was here that the first uprising against the Bourbons broke out in 1848), where a fountain is topped with the *Genio di Palermo*, a bearded figure which has become one of the city's symbols. Just off the square, on via Garibaldi, is the vast bulk of the **Palazzo di Ajutamicristo**, one of Palermo's best surviving Catalan-Gothic mansions (to stay there, see page 36).

Turn left after the palace to reach the **piazza Magione**, controversially grassed over and turned into a park in the 1990s. It's still etched with the ruins of streets flattened during the wartime raids. Overlooking the square, set in a palm-shaded garden, is the 12th-century Norman church of **La Magione** (Mon-Sat 0930-1900, Sun 0900-1330, donation requested). At the furthest end of the square, walk down **via dello Spasimo** to reach the poignant ruins of the **Chiesa di Santa Maria dello Spasimo** which are now a sublime open-air cultural centre and concert hall. Beyond it is the palm-shaded **piazza Kalsa**, a little green oasis.

For more extensive gardens, turn right down via Nicolò Cervello (the continuation of via Torremuzza) and cross the Via Lincoln to reach the gardens of the **Villa Giulia** (also known as La Flora), first laid out in the 18th century. The adjoining **Botanical Gardens** (daily 0900-1330, 1430-1900, €4, ortobotanico.palermo.it), which opened in 1795, have more than 30 acres filled with tropical plants.

to visitors. The palace was built for the Lanza-Filangeri family in the 16th century, although most of the furnishings date from the late 18th and early 19th centuries. The visit includes sumptuous public salons, a Chinese room, and a collection of historic carriages in the stables.

Chiesa di San Francesco d'Assisi
ⓘ *Piazza San Francesco d'Assisi, T091-616 2819. Daily 0800-1200, 1600-1830, free.*
Around the corner from the Palazzo Mirto, the 13th-century Chiesa di San Francesco d'Assisi boasts a fine portal and a huge rose window. The graceful interior contains the delicately sculpted *Cappella Mastrantonio* (1468), a Renaissance masterpiece by Francesco Laurana and Pietro da Bonitate. There are some sculptures by Serpotta in the nave; to see more, head to the oratory next door.

Oratorio di San Lorenzo
ⓘ *Via dell'Immacolatella (corner with piazza San Francesco d'Assisi). Daily 1000-1800, €2.*
The Oratory of San Lorenzo was built in the mid-16th century and splendidly remodelled a century or so later, when Giacomo Serpotta (1652-1732), the outstanding Rococo stucco artist, filled it with vivid depictions of events from the lives of St Lawrence and St Francis. An altarpiece depicting the Nativity, painted in 1609 by Caravaggio (1571-1610), was stolen in 1969 and has never been traced: a copy now hangs in its place. The theft of the painting has long been attributed to the Mafia, a notion backed up by information provided by *pentitos* (mafioso informers) over the years. Although many still hope that the painting will some day be returned (its notoriety means that it can't ever be sold), in 2009 an informer said that the painting had been damaged beyond repair and its remnants were buried in a garden.

Porta Felice and Foro Italico
Corso Vittorio Emanuele culminates by the seafront at the Baroque Porta Felice. From here, a modern seafront promenade, the Foro Italico, stretches along the coast.

Around La Vucciria

The eye-popping spoils of the famous Vucciria market are displayed in all their fleshy splendour along a mesh of narrow streets and squares enclosed by the via Roma and the corso Vittorio Emanuele. There are other unmissable sights here too, from sumptuous Baroque oratories to the superb archaeological museum.

Mercato della Vucciria
ⓘ *Via Roma, la Cala, piazza del Garraffello, via Argenteria nuova, piazza Caracciolo, via Maccheronai. Mon-Sat 0700-1400.*
Rumours of the demise of Palermo's oldest and most celebrated market have been rife for many years, but, even as the stall-holders lament 'the old days', it remains an exuberant, pungent, noisy spectacle. Come to see stalls of offal, the skinned heads of unidentifiable animals, enormous swordfish, and fruit and vegetables of every variety.

Chiesa di San Domenico
ⓘ *Piazza S Domenico (just off via Roma), T091-329588. Tue-Fri 0900-1130, Sat-Sun 1700-1900.*
This enormous Baroque church was completed in 1640, although the lavish façade was tacked on in 1726 when the square in front was widened to offer a better view. It's often

called Sicily's Pantheon, although few visitors will have heard of most of the worthies buried here. They include former Italian prime minister Francesco Crispi and the painter Pietro Novelli.

Oratorio del Rosario di San Domenico and Oratorio di Santa Zita (Cita)
ⓘ *Via del Bambinai/via Valverde 3, T091-332779. Mon-Sat 0900-1300, €5/4 concession, free under 6, includes admission to both oratories.*
Directly behind the Chiesa di San Domenico, the 16th-century Oratory of San Domenico is endowed with a superb altarpiece by Anton van Dyck, the *Madonna del Rosario* (1648). Giacomo Serpotta created the stucco decoration in this chapel, and the entrance ticket includes admission to his great masterpiece, the breathtaking Oratorio di Santa Zita (also known as Cita) inside the nearby church of the same name. It's impossible to hold back a gasp as you enter: the walls seem to pulse with life. The battle of Lepanto (1571) is played out vigorously on one wall, while swarms of *putti* cavort playfully around the doors. It's said that Serpotta used street urchins for his models, and his nonchalant little angels, swinging their legs in their patched boots, seem only a moment away from jumping down and skedaddling.

Museo Archeologico Regionale Salinas
ⓘ *Piazza Olivella 24, T091-611 6805. Tue-Fri 0830-1345, 1500-1845, Sat-Mon 0830-1345, €6/3 concession, free under 18 and over 60.*
Palermo's excellent archaeological museum, located at the corner of via Cavour and via Roma, contains some extraordinary ancient treasures, most gathered from the great sites of western Sicily, including Segesta, Himera and Selinunte. The best works are on the ground floor. These contain a slab of inscribed stone, part of the *Pietra di Palermo*, a 5000-year-old delivery note confirming the safe arrival of some cedar wood for the Pharaoh, which has proved invaluable for determining ancient Egyptian chronology. Other highlights include fifth-century BC water spouts in the form of lions' heads, which once adorned the Temple of Victory at Himera. Best of all are the magnificent *metopes* (stone carvings) brought from the temples of Selinunte. These carved panels were part of a long, decorative frieze and are beautifully displayed to illustrate how they might have looked 2500 years ago. The most famous carving depicts Perseus slaying the Gorgon as Athena looks on.

Upstairs, the collections continue with finds from the main archaeological sites of western Sicily, including Selinunte and Lilybaeum (modern Marsala). There are countless terracotta figures, from various sites across the island, but one room contains an eye-popping selection of votive offerings brought from the sanctuary of Demeter Malophorus at Selinunte. The top floor (not always open) contains some superb Roman mosaics.

Il Capo

The Capo district is run-down, but remains one of central Palermo's liveliest and most authentic neighbourhoods. Its life blood is the Mercato del Capo, a noisy, exuberant street market that has existed here since Palermo was Bal'harm.

Mercato del Capo
ⓘ *Porta Carini, via Sant'Agostino, via Cappuccinell.*
The market begins at the porta Carini (the oldest of the three surviving medieval gateways into the city) and fans out into surrounding side streets. As well as fresh produce, it also sells clothes, saucepans, candles, car batteries and almost anything else you can imagine.

Teatro Massimo
ⓘ *Piazza Verdi, T091-605 3580 (box office), teatromassimo.it. Guided tours (25 mins) Tue-Sun 1000-1430, €8/5 concession, held in several languages. Book guided visits on T091-605 3267.*
Palermo's opera house sits at the junction of via Maqueda and via Volturno. It was begun by Giovanni Battista Basile in 1875 and completed by his son Ernesto in 1897. Ernesto Basile, who would become the city's greatest exponent of Italian art nouveau, known as *stile Liberty*, endowed his father's splendid Neoclassical edifice with some beautiful *stile-Liberty* details. You might recognize the theatre from the *The Godfather (Part III)*.

Around via Libertà

The smartest neighbourhoods of modern Palermo unfold north of the Teatro Massimo. Another lavish 19th-century theatre overlooks the main square at piazza Ruggero Settimo, and beyond it stretches the viale della Libertà (usually known as via Libertà), now lined with chic shops. The street culminates in the refreshing gardens of the Giardino Inglese.

Piazza Ruggero Settimo
Dominated by the extravagant Teatro Politeama Garibaldi (1891), piazza Ruggero Settimo is the main hub of modern Palermo. It merges with the adjoining piazza Castelnuovo, and is commonly known as the Piazza Politeama. This is the heart of the city's smartest shopping district.

Via Libertà and the Giardino Inglese
This street, which stretches for 2½ km between Politeama and the Giardino Inglese, gets its name from the lavish *stile-Liberty* villas which bloomed in this vicinity at the turn of the 20th century. Many were destroyed by bombs during the Second World War, and many more were demolished, shamefully, during the 'Sack of Palermo' in the 1950s and 1960s. It's now the fanciest shopping street in town. The street culminates in the **Giardino Inglese** ⓘ *0900-1700, until 1800 in summer*, Palermo's loveliest public gardens, which were laid out in the 19th century. There are more charming gardens at the **Villa Trabia** (enter from the via Salinas).

Palermo fringes

On the fringes of Palermo are a string of fascinating sights, all accessible on Palermo's comprehensive public bus system, or by taxi. These range from an Arabic-style medieval palace, to a shiver-inducing crypt full of desiccated bodies.

Castello della Zisa
ⓘ *Piazza Guglielmo il Buono, T091-652 0269, summer Tue-Sat 0900-1900, Sun-Mon 0900-1330, winter daily 0900-1330, €6/3 concession, free under 18. Bus 124 from piazza Ruggero Settimo.*
The name of this exquisite palace comes from the Arabic word *al-Aziz*, meaning 'splendid', and it is the best example of Arabic-Sicilian secular architecture on the island. The Norman king William I of Sicily (1131-1166) commissioned the finest Arabic craftsmen to build the palace, which was begun around 1164 and completed for his son William II. The Ziza features richly textured vaulted arches known as *muquarnas*, as well as gilded mosaics and intricately carved capitals. The cool salons, shaded with carved wooden screens, provide an exquisite backdrop for the small collection of Islamic art – mainly ceramics and

metalwork. The most extravagant room is the **Sala della Fontana**, which once boasted an internal fountain, while outside the modern fountains and gardens provide a refreshing retreat from the heat.

Villa Malfitano
ⓘ *Via Dante 167, T091-681 6133. Mon-Sat 0900-1300, €6 house (guided visits only) and gardens. Buses 106, 108 (from piazza Politeama), 122 (from Stazione Centrale).*

This luscious, *stile-Liberty* villa set in extravagant gardens was built in 1887 by Ignazio Greco for Joseph 'Pip' Whitaker, whose family made a fortune in Marsala wine. Its gilded salons were at the centre of the social whirl at the turn of the 20th century, and visitors included several British royals. The exquisite interior can be admired on guided tours, but the blissful gardens are the real draw.

Convento dei Cappuccini
ⓘ *Via Cipressi 1, T091-212633. Daily 0900-1200, 1500-1700, €3. Bus 327.*

Beneath this nondescript church on Palermo's western outskirts is one of the creepiest and most surreal sights on the island: thousands of skeletons, all dressed up in their finery. Quite why Sicilians chose to preserve and display their dead remains a mystery. The practice was finally abandoned in 1881, but the most famous occupant arrived (illegally) in 1920: two-year-old Rosalia Lombardo lies in her glass coffin like a pretty doll, her blonde curls topped with a yellow bow.

Parco della Favorita
ⓘ *Main entrance on piazza Miscemi.*

This former 18th-century royal pleasure garden is now an extensive public park in the northern reaches of Palermo. It sits at the foot of Monte Pellegrino and contains the city's hippodrome and football stadium as well as some charming follies. Among them is the recently restored **Casina Cinese** ⓘ *T091-707 1317*, occupied in the early years of the 19th century by King Ferdinand of Naples during his enforced exile. At the **Museo Etnografico Pitrè** ⓘ *via Duca degli Abruzzi 1, T091-740 4879, Sat-Thu 0830-2000, €5*, a folklore museum named after the great Sicilian ethnologist Giuseppe Pitrè, there's a wonderful collection of Sicilian puppets, *caretti* (colourfully painted carts), costumes and musical instruments.

Palermo listings

For hotel and restaurant price codes and other relevant information, see pages 11-16.

Where to stay

Palermo *p24, map p26*

€€€€ Grand Hotel Villa Igiea, *Salita Belmonte 43, T091-631 2111, hilton.com/Italy*. A lavish art nouveau villa, designed by Ernesto Basile, this hotel sits in gardens on the edge of Palermo bay. The public salons are gorgeous, but bedrooms need updating.

€€€€ Hotel Principe di Villafranca, *Via G Turrisi Colonna 4, T091-611 8523, principedivillafranca.it*. A modern, central hotel, this was fully renovated in 2010 and offers elegant minimalist rooms and suites brightened with contemporary artworks. It's located in the upmarket shopping neighbourhood by the piazza Politeama. Off-peak deals available online can drop the price under €100 per night.

€€€ Grand Hotel et des Palmes, *Via Roma 398, T091-602 8111, hotel-despalmes.it*. This villa belonging to the Ingham-Whitaker family, was converted into a hotel in the late 19th century and then lavishly remodelled in *stile Liberty* by Ernesto Basile.

€€€ Palazzo Ajutamicristo, *Via Garibaldi 23, T091-616 1894, palazzoajutamicristo.it*. The owners offer guided tours of their 15th-century *palazzo* as well as B&B accommodation in the former servants' quarters. The rooms are comfortable and guests can breakfast on the splendid terrace.

€€€ Palazzo Conte Federico, *Via dei Biscottari 4, T091-651 1881, contefederico.com*. Another sumptuous palace tucked away in the old quarter, this dates back to the 12th century, although most of what exists today is from the 17th and 18th centuries. The count and countess offer B&B rooms that retain their original beams but are otherwise simply furnished.

€€ BB22, *Palazzo Pantelleria, Largo Cavalieri di Malta 22, T091-611 1610, bb22.it*. Perhaps the most stylish B&B in the city, with a handful of beautifully designed bedrooms which mix neo-Baroque chandeliers with chrome. It's next to the church of San Domenico, but ongoing neighbourhood restoration may mean unwanted noise. There's no lift.

€€-€ Ambasciatori Hotel, *Via Roma 111, T091-616 6881, ambasciatorihotelpalermo.net*. This modest, three-star hotel is family-run and perfectly located in the heart of the city. While it may not have oodles of character, it does offer immaculate rooms, charming service, and a roof terrace (where breakfast is served) for splendid views.

€ B&B Palazzo Reale, *Via Cappuccini 9, T091-424045, bbpalazzoreale.it*. A smart little B&B very near the Norman Palace, with just three individually styled bedrooms. Bright, colourful and modern, it's one of the best bets in the city if you're looking for style on a budget.

€ Sole Luna della Solidarietà B&B, *Via Vincenzo Riolo 7, T091-581671, solelunabedandbreakfast.org*. This friendly little B&B can be found near the Teatro Politeama, about a five-minute walk from the central via Roma. It's run by delightful Patrizia, who spent years working with deprived children in Palermo (5% of the profits from the B&B goes to the children's charity Arciragazzi). No credit cards.

€ Giorgio's House, *Via A Mongitore, T091-525057, giorgioshouse.com*. Effervescent and irrepressible, Giorgio is a Palermitan fixture. His budget B&B is colourful and pristine, and he can't do enough for his guests, providing a free pick-up service at the train station, and happily dispensing insider tips on where to eat and what to do.

Self-catering

28 Butera, *28 via Butera, T333-316 5432, butera28.it*. Avid fans of *The Leopard* can stay in Giuseppe di Lampedusa's former home, which has been lovingly restored by his nephew. The upper levels of the house have been divided into comfortable self-catering apartments. Prices start at €50 per day/€330 per week for a studio apartment, rising to €120 per day/€770 per week for the largest apartment with terrace. Cooking lessons with the Duchess of Palma can be arranged.

€€ **Chez Jasmine**, *Vicolo dei Nassaiuoli 15, T091-616 4268, chezjasmine.biz*. This little hideaway is at the top of a *palazzo* in the Kalsa district. The apartment is split over two levels, linked by a spiral staircase, and there's also a pretty little roof terrace (€110-130 per night for two people). Minimum stay of three nights.

Restaurants

Palermo *p24, map p26*

€€€€ **Cin Cin**, *Via Manin 22, T091-612 4095, ristorantecincin.com. Mon-Sat 1230-1500, 2000-2300, lunch only Jul-Aug*. 'Sicilian Baroque' cuisine is the speciality at this restaurant. This translates into traditional recipes such as *spaccatelle* with pesto Ericino, or fresh fish of the day served with mussels and clams.

€€€ **Cucina**, *Via Principe di Villafranca 54, Palermo, T0916-268416*. Currently one of the city's hottest addresses, chef Roberto Giannettino prepares updated versions of Sicilian classics. The menu changes regularly in order to reflect what's in season, but might include dishes like the Palermitan classic, *pasta con de sarde*, or *macco*, a spring soup made of fresh baby broad beans.

€€€ **Kursaal Kalhesa**, *Via Foro Umberto Primo 121, T091-616 2111. Tue-Sat 1200-1500, 1900-0130, Sun 1200-0130*. In a stunning medieval *palazzo* in the Kalsa district, this restaurant boasts a beautiful summer terrace, set in a 'secret' courtyard. Dine on market-fresh, seasonal cuisine, which might include grilled vegetables topped with smoked cheese or tenderloin in Sicilian wine.

€€€ **La Cambusa**, *Piazza Marina 16, T091-584574, lacambusa.it. Mon 1930-2300, Tue-Sun 1230-1500, 1930-2300*. Looks deceive at this apparently simple little restaurant, which is renowned for its fresh fish. Book early to get a seat on the plant-fringed terrace. Start with the seafood salad and follow up with simply grilled sea bass – or whatever is fresh that day.

€€€ **Piccolo Napoli**, *Piazzetta Mulino a Vento 4, T091-320431. Mon-Thu 1230-1530, Fri-Sat 1230-1530, 2000-2230*. A reliable, traditional restaurant about a five-minute walk from the Teatro Politeama, with a spectacular seafood display at the entrance. Everything here is seasonal and fresh, from the antipasti to the fish and shellfish.

€€€ **Sant'Andrea**, *Piazza Sant'Andrea 4, T091-334999. Mon-Sat 2000-2330*. Book in advance for this rustically furnished trattoria in the Vucciria neighbourhood which prepares excellent Sicilian cuisine. Try the outstanding *pasta con le sarde*, a Sicilian classic made with fresh sardines, wild fennel, pine nuts and raisins, and finish up with home-made desserts.

€€ **Il Maestro del Brodo**, *Via Pannieri, T091-329523. Tue-Sun 1300-1500, 1930-2230*. On the fringes of Vucciria, this traditional tavern draws locals and tourists alike with its good value menu of Palermitani favourites. Try the spaghetti with sea urchins and *neonata* (tiny baby fish) and the seafood mixed grill (*grigliata mista*).

€€ **Il Mirto e la Rosa**, *Via Principe de Granatelli 30, T091-324353, ilmirtoelarosa. com. Mon-Sat 1230-1500, 1930-2300*. This vaulted restaurant also serves as an art gallery. The menu changes according to what's freshest in the market.

€€ **Ristorante Risi e Bisi**, *Vicolo Gesù e Maria a Palazzo Reale 15, T091-652 1037. Tue-Sun 1200-1500, 1900-2300*. Just a stone's throw from the Palazzo dei Normanni, this restaurant specializes in fish and seafood. The menu changes, but, if available, you should try the risotto with prawns and champagne.

€€ Trattoria ai Cascinari, *Via d'Ossuna 43-45, T091-651 9804. Tue, Wed, Sun 1300-1500, 1930-2300, Thu-Sat 1930-2300.* A great place for lunch after a stroll through the Capo market, this buzzy trattoria celebrates Palermo's delicious specialities. Try *sarde a beccafico* (sardines stuffed with breadcrumbs, pine nuts, and lemon) and follow up with a plate of home-made pasta or some fresh fish.

€€-€ Pizzeria Bellini, *Piazza Bellini 6, T091-616 5691. Tue-Sun 1230-1500, 1930-2300.* There are always queues at this relaxed, family-run trattoria, with a terrace in front of the cupolas of La Martorana and San Cataldo. In the evenings, outstanding pizzas are on the menu, but there's also a good range of pasta, fish and meat dishes.

€ Antica Focacceria San Francesco, *Via Paternostro 58, T091-320264, afsf.it.* This is the place to get your *pane con la milza* (veal spleen sandwiches), with focaccia offered for less adventurous palates. It's been going since 1834, and the family owners are currently in the news after refusing to pay the Mafia *pizzo* (the police car at the door is for their protection).

€ La Maschere, *Via Vaglica 4, T091-335622.* This simple pizzeria near the Teatro Massimo is a big favourite with young Palermitani thanks to its cosy wood-panelled interior, reliably good pizzas and salads, and bargain prices. They also serve a selection of meat and fish dishes.

Cafés and bars

Aboriginal Internet Café, *Via Spinuzza 51, T091-662 2229, aboriginalcafe.com. Daily 1000-0300.* A friendly, colourful café. Internet access costs a very reasonable €3.50 per hour, and includes free coffee.

Bar Alba, *Piazza Don Bosco 7c, T091-309016, baralba.it. Tue-Sun 0700-2200, Sat 0700-2400, daily in summer.* The coffee served at this unassuming modern café is regularly voted the best in Italy. Try it for yourself with a pastry, ice cream or freshly made *arancine*.

Caffè Cappello, *Via Colonna Rotta 68, T091-489 9601. Daily 0800–2200.* A smart tea room and pastry shop serving all kinds of delicious local cakes, pastries and biscuits, which is famous for its pralines. Modern and stylish, and handily placed for a break from shopping along the via Libertà.

Caffè Spinnato, *Via Principe del Belmonte 107-115, T091-583231. Daily 0700-2100.* Sit out at an umbrella-shaded table on the summer terrace at this legendary café, and order from the extensive menu.

Golosandia, *Corso Vittorio Emanuele 101, T091-611 5082. Summer daily 1000-2200, reduced hours in winter.* This artisanal gelateria, just off piazza Marina, is a member of *Addio Pizzo*, so treat yourself with an extra large helping of the heavenly *nocciola* (hazelnut).

Ilardo, *Foro Italico 11-12, T091-616 4413. Summer daily 1100-2200, winter weekends only.* The city's oldest gelateria, founded in 1860, enjoys a seafront location.

Taverna Azzurra, *Via Domenico Scina 121, T091-583541. Mon-Sat 0900-2200.* It's always a squeeze at this traditional tavern in the Vucciria market, but well worth the effort for a draught of beer to wash down the street-food snacks.

Entertainment

Palermo *p24, map p26*
Children
As well as the beaches, parks, castles, ice cream shops and pizzerias, most children will enjoy Sicilian puppet theatres (although he stories are usually too gory for younger kids). Recommended theatres include the following:

Teatro di Mimmo Cuticchio, *Via Bara all'Olivello 95, Palermo, T091-323400, figlidartecuticchio.com.* This puppet theatre and workshop is run by one of Palermo's most celebrated and accomplished theatrical families.

Teatro di Ippogrifo, *Vicolo Ragusi 6, Palermo, T091-329194.*

Teatroarte-Cuticchio, *Via del Benedettini 9, T091-323400, teatroarte-cuticchio.com.*

Clubs

Al 5 La Tavernetta, *Via Dei Chiavettieri 5. Wed-Mon 1800-0300, T328-852 5281.* A lively spot for cocktails or an aperitif accompanied by tasty snacks and light meals. Upbeat music, a friendly crowd and the occasional live gig.

I Candelai, *Via Candelai 65, Palermo, T091-327151. Daily 2100-0300, usually free.* One of the city's first clubs, on a street now filled with bars and pubs, this still offers nightly entertainment in the form of live gigs or massive DJ sessions.

Kursaal Kalhesa, *Via Foro Umberto Primo 121, Palermo, T091-616 2111. Daily 1900-0300.* This boho-chic haunt is a great place to start the night. Sit beneath the vaults of this medieval *palazzo* and enjoy a drink. Upstairs is a restaurant, see above.

La Cuba, *Viale Francesco Scaduto 12, Palermo, T091-309201. Lounge bar open daily 1900 till late.* This lounge bar and club is found in the Villa Sperlinga halfway between the Giardino Inglese and the Parco della Favorita. This is where the beautiful people come, so dress up.

MiKalsa Bar, *Via Torremuzza 27, Palermo, T348-973 2254. Tue-Thu 2030-0100, Fri-Sat 2030-0200, mikalsa.it.* A stylish option in the Kalsa neighbourhood, with live gigs, and an enormous selection of international beers. Programme available online.

Music

Teatro Massimo, *Piazza G Verdi, Palermo, T091-605 3580, teatromassimo.it.* Palermo's opera house offers a superb programme of ballet and opera.

Teatro Garibaldi 'Politeama', *Piazza Ruggero Settimo, Palermo, T091-605 3421.* This grand 19th-century theatre is a major venue for classical music. Major restoration began in 2011, so check in advance if open.

Festivals and events

Palermo *p24, map p26*
Kals'Art festival. *Jul-Aug.* This summer cultural festival takes place in the Kalsa district, with theatre, dance, concerts, film screenings and more. It also has a winter edition, held in late December.

Festino di Santa Rosalia. *10-15 Jul.* A five-day celebration dedicated to Palermo's patron saint.

Shopping

Palermo *p24, map p26*
Beachwear and clothing

Giglio Donna, *Piazza Francesco Crispi 3, T091-611 4102, giglio.com. Mon-Sat 1000-1300, 1630-2000.* Giglio have hip boutiques around the city. This is the cool, pale, designer establishment for women – just the place to pick out that little black dress you'll need to party with the well-dressed Sicilians. They also have an amazing children's shoe shop on the same square.

Food and drink

For picnic supplies, you'll be spoilt for choice at Palermo's three street markets – Ballarò, Vucciria and Capo, see page 25, page 32, and page 33 respectively.

Enoteca Picone di Palermo, *Via Marconi 36, Palermo, T091-331300, enotecapicone.it. Mon-Sat 0730-1400, 1600-2100. Closed Aug.* Perhaps the finest and most extensive wine selection in the city, which also doubles as a superb gourmet wine bar.

I Sapori e i Saperi della Legalità, *Piazza Castelnuovo 13, Palermo, T091-322023, liberaterra.it. Mon-Sat 1000-1400, 1700-2000.* An *alimentari* (food shop) dedicated to the organic products grown on estates confiscated from the Mafia through the Libera Terra organisation.

L'Emporio, *Corso Vittorio Emanuele 172, Palermo, T329-091 7791. Mon-Sat 1000-1230, 1700-2000.* This unique gift shop cum grocery store is stocked with *pizzo*-free products: blood orange honey, organic olive oil as well as anti-Mafia slogan T-shirts.

Outdoor equipment
Adventure Time, *Via Volturno 27, Palermo, T091-611 8857, adventuretime.it. Mon 1530-2000, tue-Sat 0900-1300 and 1530-2000.* Everything you need to enjoy the great outdoors at this centrally located shop.

What to do

Palermo *p24, map p26*
Cultural
City Sightseeing, *T091-589429, palermo.city-sightseeing.it*. A hop on, hop off open-topped sightseeing bus makes the circuit of central Palermo and Monreale with a multilingual audio commentary. Tours depart roughly every 20 minutes/1 hour (depending on the season) from near the Teatro Politeama.
Real Sicily, *T347-480 9632, realsicily.com*. Marcella Amato is an experienced and multilingual guide who offers individual and small group tours in Palermo and the surrounding area. Cookery classes and visits to wineries can also be arranged.

Food and wine
Ristorante Cin Cin, *Via Manin 22, Palermo, T091-612 4095, ristorantecincin.com*. This prestigious restaurant (see page 37) offers one-day cooking classes, which include a visit to the market to choose ingredients, then the preparation of the feast. €150 per person in small groups of two to eight.

Transport

Palermo *p24, map p26*
Bus
There's no central bus station, but the main regional and inter-urban services stop near the train station, mostly along via Balsamo and via Gregorio.

AMAT (T848-800817, amat.pa.it) runs a comprehensive network of local buses. Buy tickets from bars and shops with the AMAT ticket before boarding for €1.30, or onboard at €1.70. Tickets cover 90 minutes of journey time, including transfers. Most buses start from the train station, or the piazza Indipendenza behind the Royal Palace. A one-way ticket costs €3.50.

The airport bus leaves from piazza Giulio Cesare (by the train station) and piazza Ruggero Settimo (by the Teatro Politeama).

Train
Stazione Centrale, piazza Stazione, T091-617 5451, to the south of the Kalsa district.
Palermo's so-called 'Metro' is actually an above-ground railway line: Metro Line A, also called the Trinacria Express, links the city centre with the airport, while the very short Metro Line B (Stazione Notarbartolo to piazza Giachery) is not useful for tourists. Line C (under construction) will head south to Termini Imerese.

Directory

Palermo *p24, map p26*
Banks ATMs everywhere, including along via Roma and via Libertà. **Banco di Sicilia**, via Roma 185, T091-331249, and via Libertà 46, T091-625 4334.
Medical services **Ospedale Generale**, via Messina Marine 197, T091-479111, ospedalebuccherilaferla.it. Several pharmacies around via Roma, including **Farmacia delle Poste** (via Roma 323, T091-584067, Mon-Fri 0900-1230, 1630-2000, Sat 0900-1230). **Post office** Via Roma 320, T091-753 5183, poste.it (Tue-Sat 0800-1830). **Tourist information** Information booths at piazza Politeama, piazza Marina and the train station (Mon-Thu 0900-1400, 1500-1900, Fri-Sat 0830-2030, Sun 0900-1300, 1500-1900). The freephone tourist information line is T800-234169 (Italian only). The main provincial tourist office is at piazza Castelnuovo 34, T091-583847.

40 • Palermo & around Palermo Listings

Around Palermo

A string of very different sights surrounds Palermo, from the seaside delights of Mondello to the magnificent Norman cathedral at Monreale. Inland is Piana degli Albanesi, which retains the unique customs of its Albanian forebears, and the hill town of Corleone, forever linked in the popular imagination with *The Godfather* films. To the east, Bagheria is still dotted with elegant Baroque mansions, and beyond it, on a headland overlooking the sea, are the serene ruins of ancient Solunto. East again, the seaside town of Cefalù, curled around the base of a massive cliff, is justly considered one of the island's most beautiful towns.

North of Palermo → *For listings, see pages 49-54.*

Mondello
ⓘ *12 km north of Palermo.*

Seaside Mondello, linked by regular local buses, is curved around a perfect bay with a sandy beach. It's been a popular resort since the late 19th century, when it was transformed from a fishing village into a chic summer retreat for wealthy Palermitani. It is still strewn with lavish villas.

Monte Pellegrino and Grotto dell'Addaura
ⓘ *14 km north of Palermo.*

The great mountain that dominates Palermo's wide bay is topped by a sanctuary dedicated to the city's beloved patron saint, Santa Rosalia. On Sundays, families drive up to picnic near the sanctuary and enjoy views. On the northern side of the mountain is the **Grotta dell'Addaura** ⓘ *T091-671 6066, closed indefinitely*, famous for its prehistoric cave paintings, which provide the earliest evidence of human settlement in the Palermo area.

South of Palermo → *For listings, see pages 49-54.*

Piana degli Albanesi
ⓘ *24 km south of Palermo.*

This tranquil town was founded in 1488 by Albanian immigrants, and the inhabitants have preserved their dialect, customs, and Orthodox religious rites. Signposts are in Albanian and Italian, and the cake shops are full of unusual Albanian goodies. The town is famous for its Easter celebrations, featuring embroidered costumes, examples of which can be seen in the **Museo Civico** ⓘ *via Guzzetta, Tue, Thu and Sat 0930-1300 and 1600-1900, Wed and Fri 0930-1300, Sun 1000-1300, free*. Peek into the 15th-century Chiesa di San Giorgio, the town's oldest church, to see the iconostasis with its gilded icons. About 4 km southwest of Piana degli Albanesi is the mountain pass where the **Portella della Ginestra** massacre took place.

Corleone
ⓘ *60 km south of Palermo.*

Nowhere in Sicily is more associated with the Mafia than Corleone, about 60 km from Palermo, reached by a potholed country road. Millions know Corleone's name thanks to Mario Puzo's novel *The Godfather*, on which Coppola based his celebrated film trilogy, but the town has long been home to one of Sicily's most important Mafia families and once had the highest murder rate in the world. The town inhabitants are fed up with this association and have opened a museum and anti-Mafia documentation centre in an attempt to shatter the stereotypes and fight against the Mafia. However, it is under threat owing to insufficient funds. If you find it open (ask at the tourist office on the main square, piazza Falcone Giovanni e Borsellino Paolo, T091-846-3655), the photographs showing Mafia victims are a grim reminder that the realities of Cosa Nostra are a world apart from the glamorous rogues portrayed by Hollywood. There's little else to do, apart from perhaps a quick look at the **Museo Civico** ⓘ *Palazzo Provenzano, via Orfanotrofio, T091-846 4907, Mon-Sat 0930-1300, 1530-1930, Sun 0930-1300, free*, which occupies a fine 15th-century *palazzo*.

If you're driving from Palermo (there's no public transport), you could drop in to the **Palazzo Reale di Ficuzza** (signposted off the SS118, 8 km north of Corleone). This late-

18th-century royal hunting lodge now contains a museum dedicated to the reserve's flora and fauna. It is also the starting point for several easy walking trails through the **Bosco di Ficuzza** (parks.it/riserva.bosco.ficuzza), Sicily's most extensive forest, and a nature reserve.

Cattedrale di Monreale

ⓘ *Piazza Duomo, Monreale, T091-640 4413, cattedraledimonreale.it. Cathedral 0830-1245, 1530-1800, free; Treasury 0900-1215, 1530-1730, €3; Cloister Mon-Sat 0930-1900, Sun 0900-1230, €6/3, audioguide €5. Bus 389 from Piazza Indipendenza, behind Palazzo dei Normanni.*

Hilltop Monreale is just a 20-minute bus ride from the centre of Palermo, and provides a peaceful retreat from the city chaos below. The meandering lanes and alleys are a delight to explore but all roads lead back to the celebrated cathedral, one of the finest Norman churches anywhere, which is still the heart of the town.

The cathedral was begun in 1174 by William II of Sicily who proclaimed that the Virgin Mary had come to him in a vision and asked that a church be built in her honour. (In reality, William II sought to curb the power of his former tutor, Gualtiero Offamiglio, the Archbishop of Palermo, by building a cathedral to outshine anything the capital could offer.) It was almost complete by 1182, an incredible feat for the age. The finest artists and craftsmen from around the Mediterranean were gathered to create this masterpiece of Sicilian Romanesque, which is an exquisite fusion of Arabic, Byzantine and Norman decorative techniques. The exterior barely hints at the magnificence within: step inside, and the impact is quite literally dazzling. The lofty nave and its supporting columns are completely encrusted with gleaming mosaics, which culminate in the huge Christ Pantocrater (Christ in Majesty) which entirely fills the apse. Among the saints and apostles ranked beneath Christ is the first image of an English saint, Thomas à Becket, who was canonized in 1174, only four years after his murder was instigated by William II's own father-in-law, Henry II. William II can be seen, on the curved wall on the left transept, being crowned by Christ, in a deliberate echo of the mosaic depiction of his father Roger II's coronation in La Martorana (see page 29). On the right transept, he is seen handing the cathedral to Mary.

Several royal tombs, including those belonging to William II, his mother Margaret of Navarre, and his father William I ('the bad`) of Sicily, are found within the cathedral. A chapel contains an urn said to hold the entrails of King Louis IX, the only canonized king of France, who died in Tunis in 1270. The most lavish of the cathedral's reliquaries can be seen in the Treasury, which also displays some richly embroidered vestments. For giddy but far-reaching views (not for the faint-hearted), you can climb the steps to the cathedral roof.

Along with the cathedral, the astonishingly beautiful cloister is all that is left of the 12th-century Benedictine monastery. There are 228 paired columns (with four columns at each of the corners), all with exquisitely sculpted capitals and reliefs, or richly gilded mosaic inserts. They are utterly enchanting, each miniature scene breathing life and vitality. In one corner, there is a fountain, which looks like a palm tree stripped of its fronds, where the monks would wash their hands.

Coast towards Cefalù

Bagheria

ⓘ *18 km east of Palermo.*

Designed as a model Baroque town in the 18th century, Bagheria was once an elegant enclave of aristocratic *palazzi* and graceful villas. Now, however, concrete development threatens to choke its elegant core, and many of the villas are sadly neglected. Some, however, have been preserved, including most famously the **Villa Palagonia** ⓘ *T091-932 088, villapalagonia.it, daily Nov-Mar 0900-1300, 1530-1730, Apr-Oct 0900-1300, 1600-1900, €5*, the only place in Sicily that Goethe really hated. Begun in 1715, the palace is a classic example of the Sicilian Baroque style – but for one major difference: the exterior walls and parapets are covered with an eye-popping array of stone monsters, which cavort eerily across the garden walls. Part of the interior can also be visited.

Shake off the memory of the grotesques at Bagheria's light-hearted toy museum, the **Museo del Giocattolo** ⓘ *via Consolare 105, T091-943801, Tue-Fri 0900-1300, 1600-1830, Sat-Sun 0900-1300, museodelgiocattolo.org, €4, €2 children aged 4-6, free under 4*, where over 700 toys spanning four centuries are housed in the 18th-century Villa Aragona Cutò. The **Museo Guttuso** ⓘ *via Rammacca 9, T091-943902, winter Tue-Sun 0900-1300, 1430-1900, summer daily 0930-1400, 1500-1900, museoguttuso.it, €5/4 concession, free under 6*, in the Villa Cattolica, is dedicated to the works of the most celebrated 20th-century Sicilian painter, Renato Guttuso (1911-1987), and other contemporary Sicilian artists.

Solunto
ⓘ *Via Collegio Romano, Località Solunto, Santa Flavia, T091-904557. Mon-Sat 0900-1730, Sun 0900-1300, €2/1 concession. Train from Palermo to Santa Flavia (€2.25, 20 mins), then walk 2 km uphill.*

On the slopes of a gentle hill, about 20 km east of Palermo, ancient Solus overlooks the sea near the fishing village of **Porticello** (which has a fantastic daily fish market). It was one of the three main Phoenician settlements on the island, but fell to the Greeks at the end of the fourth century BC, when it became a satellite of Himera (see below). Most of what survives dates from the Roman colony of Soluntum which developed here from the third century BC. There isn't much to see, but it's a peaceful and atmospheric spot, and the views across the undulating coastline are wonderful. Some of the finds are displayed in a small museum at the entrance.

Termini Imerese
ⓘ *39 km east of Palermo.*

Termini Imerese is an ancient spa town with a delightful old centre, where you can still take the waters at the 19th-century Grand Hotel delle Terme (see page 53). The town is split in two, with the old village (Termini Alta) arranged in terraces on a rocky promontory and a modern resort (Termini Bassa) splayed along the beach below. The focus of the old town is the 15th-century Duomo, which overlooks the main square. Nearby the **Museo Civico** ⓘ *via Marco Tullio Cicerone, T091-812 8550, Tue-Sat 0900-1300, 1600-1830, Sun 0800-1230, free*, contains finds from the ancient Greek city of Himera (see below). Don't miss the wonderful coastal views from the Principe di Piemonte Belvedere, near the cathedral.

Himera
ⓘ *Contrada Buonfornello, T091-814 0128. Mon-Sat 0900 till 1 hr before sunset, Sun 0900-1330, €2/1 concession. Just off the SS113 (or take the Buonfornello exit on the A19 motorway), 12 km east of Termini Imerese. Randazzo buses (T091-814 8235), run a twice-daily bus service to Himera; check times with tourist offices in advance.*

Confronted by a straggle of stones lost in sun-bleached grass, it requires some imaginative effort to recreate the once powerful Greek colony that occupied this site. Himera was founded in 648 BC by Greek colonists from Zankle (modern Messina), but was dangerously close to the Carthaginian settlement at Solunto, just 30 km away. In 480 BC, the Carthaginians attacked Himera but the invaders were repelled by an enormous Greek army that included troops from Agrigento and Syracuse. The Carthaginian army was led by the famous general Hamilcar, whose grandson Hannibal led a second attack on Himera in 409 BC. This time, the Carthaginians were victorious: Himera was utterly destroyed, and its inhabitants slaughtered or deported. The only substantial ruins to survive are those of the **Tempio della Vittoria** (Temple of Victory), which celebrated the Greek victory of 480 BC. Himera hit the news in 2008, when a vast necropolis was discovered containing more than 10,000 skeletons, including adults, children and babies (the babies, touchingly, were buried with their 'bottles').

Caccamo
ⓘ *14 km south of Termini Imerese.*

The little town of Caccamo is set on the northeastern slopes of Monte San Calogero (1326 m), which rises dramatically from the coastal plain, making it appear considerably higher than it is in reality. Dominating the town is its fabulous medieval castle, the **Castello di Caccamo** ⓘ *via Termitana, daily 0900-1230, 1500-1830/1600-2000 in summer, €2*, with its fairy tale crenellations and ramparts. The interior has been substantially remodelled and only a small section is open to the public, but the views from the ramparts are particularly outstanding.

Cefalù → *For listings, see pages 49-54.*

If you had to invent the perfect Sicilican seaside town, chances are it would look just like Cefalù. The red roofs of the old town are huddled around a golden cathedral, painted wooden boats are drawn up on the sands, a glorious beach stretches seemingly forever; and an enormous castle-topped rock provides a dramatic backdrop. In August, this stretch of coast is busy, but, fortunately, escape is on hand in the form of the verdant peaks of Madonie mountains. Sicily's highest mountain range, now an extensive natural park, stretches inland south of Cefalù. Scattered across the hills are old-fashioned towns and villages, mostly dedicated to the traditions of rearing livestock and cultivating olives and other crops. It's the perfect location if you're looking for a walking, riding or mountain-biking holiday, with some wonderful *agriturismi* offering a range of activities.

Cefalù's charming, perfectly preserved historic centre is presided over by a beautiful cathedral containing some of the finest Byzantine mosaics in Europe. Lively beaches extend along the coast, with a host of blaring discos and restaurants in summer, but you can escape the crowds by making the stiff climb up La Rocca. This massive headland boasts stunning views in all directions.

Duomo
ⓘ *Piazza del Duomo, T0921-922021. Summer 0800-1200, 1530-1830, winter 0800-1200, 1530-1700, free.*

Cefalù's golden cathedral rises serenely above the red-tiled roofs of the old town. It was built, according to local legend, to honour a promise made by the Norman count and future king of Sicily, Roger II (1130-1154), whose ship survived a terrible storm to land virtually unscathed on Cefalù's beach. Constructed between 1131 and 1267, the original, grandiose plans were substantially scaled down after Roger's death in 1154. Nonetheless, the cathedral remains one of the finest in Sicily.

Its restrained beauty is infused with just a hint of menace: the cathedral was begun, after all, just a year after Roger II was crowned King of Sicily, when he was still unsure where the loyalties of his new subjects lay. The fortress-like exterior stands testament to the might of the king. The façade is flanked with a pair of sturdy Norman towers, each topped with a pointed steeple added in the 15th century. Behind it rises the sheer face of La Rocca. It's a stunning picture, which you can drink up over a coffee or a glass of wine at one of the numerous terrace cafés on the piazza del Duomo.

Through the heavy doors, the vaulted interior is dimly lit, but the impact of the glittering Byzantine mosaics above the main altar is undiminished by the gloom. Dominating the entire apse is the huge, unusually benign, image of Christ Pantocrator (Christ the All-Powerful) his right hand raised in blessing. Christ's gaze – steady and deeply compassionate – is incredibly humane and lifelike. Beneath the Christ figure is a sensitively rendered Virgin Mary, in robes of dazzling blue, flanked on either side by archangels. Beneath her are the Twelve Apostles, each minutely rendered in shimmering tiles. These sublime mosaics were created between 1148 and 1170 by master craftsmen specially summoned from Greece and Constantinople, and are among the earliest and best preserved on the island. Near the belfry, a door leads to the graceful 12th-century cloister, with its pairs of slender columns carved with fabulous beasts.

Museo Mandralisca

ⓘ *Via Mandralisca 12, T0921-421547, fondazionemandralisca.it. Daily 0900-1900, until 2300 in Aug, €5/3 concession, children under 6 free, €1 children 6-10, €3 children 11-15.*

The Baron of Mandralisca (1809-1864) was a politician, philanthropist, amateur archaeologist, and passionate mollusc fan. While his extensive collection of shells (more than 20,000 at the last count) and cabinets full of stuffed animals will leave most visitors cold, the Baron's magpie instincts did lead him to acquire two outstanding masterpieces. The first is a Greek vase from the fourth century BC, painted with a comical scene of a fishmonger hacking away at a large fish as his customer quakes before him. The second is a masterly portrait by Sicilian Antonello da Messina (1430-1479), *Portrait of an Unknown Man* (1470), which depicts its sitter slyly gazing out at the viewer with an enigmatic smile. Only a few dozen examples of this accomplished painter's work survive, most of them found in the world's great museums, making it all the more extraordinary that such a splendid painting is on display in the provincial Museo Mandralisca.

Città vecchia

Shop-lined corso Ruggero is the main street of the worn yet charming *città vecchia* (old town), which is laid out in a simple grid pattern and scattered with handsome old buildings. The finest of these is the 13th-century **Osteria Magno** (corner of corso Ruggero and via Amendola), traditionally (if erroneously) believed to have been occupied by Roger II, and now restored and used for occasional exhibitions. Perhaps the most atmospheric corner of the old town is the little beach, where fishing boats are perfectly framed by the ancient **Porta Marina**, the only surviving gateway in the medieval walls. Colourfully painted boats are pulled up onto the strand, from where you'll enjoy enchanting views of the town in the shadow of the great rock.

La Rocca

The vast rock that dominates the town can be reached via a steep flight of steps from buzzing piazza Garibaldi. Huff and puff your way to the top (it takes roughly an hour, bring plenty of water) for stunning views. There are few vestiges of the settlements that crowned this rock before the Normans built their town at the base of the headland. The best preserved is the **Tempio di Diana** (Temple of Diana), a megalithic construction of pale cubes dating back to the ninth century BC, adapted four centuries later and dedicated to the goddess of the hunt and the moon. Little survives of the recently restored, once-mighty Arab fortress that so impressed early travellers, but the views over the red-tiled rooftops and the cathedral far below are unforgettable.

Beaches

The *lungomare* stretches from the old town all the way along Cefalù's modern extension, which spreads along the city's main beach. The beach is crammed in summer, and access is almost entirely limited to expensive lidos: the further you walk from town, the cheaper they get. It's a good family beach, with shallow waters. Locals prefer the pebbly Caldura beach (on the eastern side of town, beyond the harbour), which is prettier and less crowded but has considerably fewer facilities. If you've got your own transport, you could head out to the lovely little beaches around Mazzaforno, 5 km from Cefalù, or the check out the surfing on the 15km-long Capo Playa which stretches west from Cefalù.

Around Cefalù → *For listings, see pages 49-54.*

The coastal resort of **Castel di Tusa** ⓘ *27 km east of Cefalù*, is famous for its collection of enormous contemporary sculptures, the *Fiumara d'Arte* (Rivers of Art), which are scattered around the town (you'll need a car to visit them all).

The 18th-century **Santuario di Gibilmanna** ⓘ *open daily 0730-1300, 1515-1930, free*, enjoys stunning views over the Madonie mountains and out to sea. It contains one of Sicily's most venerated statues, an image of the Madonna credited with numerous miracles, which is the focus of an enormous pilgrimage every year on 8 September. There are lots of good picnic spots under the surrounding trees.

The **Parco delle Madonie** is named after the Madonie mountain range, this beautiful 40,000-ha natural park encompasses forest-covered mountains dotted with medieval villages and traditional farmsteads. In summer, the park's meadows are carpeted with wild orchids, and an extraordinary variety of butterflies dance in the sunlight. In winter, skiing can be enjoyed for a few weeks in January and February. **Castelbuono**, the principal town in the Madonie and one of its most beautiful, tumbles magically down a hillside, its steep streets of rosy stone crowned by a **medieval castle** ⓘ *May-Sep Tue-Sun 0830-1400, 1600-1900, Oct-Apr Tue-Sun 0900-1300, 1500-2000, €2*. Little **Collesano** has a splendid Gothic Duomo, and a smattering of medieval churches. A ski resort is the last thing you might expect to find in Sicily, but **Piano Battaglia**, complete with Alpine-style chalets, is just that. Perched at around 1600 m, it's surprisingly popular, and also attracts plenty of walkers during the summer months. Tucked away in the south of the park, lofty **Petralia Soprana** and its neighbour **Petralia Sottana** are two of the loveliest and best-preserved medieval towns in the Madonie, with wonderful views stretching all the way to Etna on clear days.

Ustica → *For listings, see pages 49-54.*

The tiny volcanic island of Ustica, floating 60 km north of Palermo, provides an ideal contrast to the mayhem of the Sicilian capital. Once a pirate lair and then a prison (right up until the 1950s), the island is now a popular, but deliciously slow-paced, tourist destination.

A mecca for divers, Ustica is protected as a marine reserve, and the turquoise coves are also perfect for snorkelling and swimming.

Ustica town
Most of the 1300 inhabitants of Ustica live in this small town, its multi-hued houses arranged in neat rows around the port. There's only one main street, which winds up from the port to the Chiesa Madre, passing colourful murals painted by artists in the 1970s. Most of the cafés, shops, bars and restaurants are concentrated around piazza Umberto I, focus of the evening *passeggiata*. On a cliff overlooking the port, the Torre Santa Maria, formerly a watchtower and prison, is now a small archaeology museum, with underwater finds. An easy path leads up to the ruined Castello Saraceno, for stunning views.

Around the island
Ustica is greener than might be expected of a volcanic island, and much of it is tamed by cultivated fields. A single road makes the 9-km journey around the island, but the interior is criss-crossed with mule tracks, which are perfect for gentle walks. A coastal path winds from Ustica town along the northern half of the island for about 4 km to reach the Punta di Megna. The whole island is a marine reserve, but it is divided into three zones with varying degrees of protection: the Punta di Megna is the northern boundary of Zone A, the most highly protected section of the reserve. Boats are prohibited, and swimming is only allowed in two small areas. The best way to see Ustica is by boat: fisherman at the harbour offer daily boat tours to coves, with black lava rocks reflected in translucent waters.

Around Palermo listings

For hotel and restaurant price codes and other relevant information, see pages 11-16.

Where to stay

Around Palermo *p41*

€€ Casale del Principe, *Contrada Dammusi, Monreale, T091-857 9910, casaledelprincipe.it*. This working farm between Monreale and San Giuseppe Jato offers elegant rooms (three of which have stunning private terraces) with views over vines and orchards. Their own produce is served in the restaurant, and activities include hiking, horse riding and archery.

€€ Villa Cefalà, *SS113 No 48, T091-931545, Santa Flavia, T091-931545, tenutacefala.it*. This *agriturismo* sits in hills near the village of Santa Flavia, a 30-minute drive east of Palermo. It offers a selection of beautifully decorated rooms, suites, or self-catering apartments. There's a pool, and restaurant serving the estate's own produce.

€ Domus Notari, *Via Duca degli Abruzzi 3, Monreale, T091-640 2550, domusnotari.it*. Tucked away in the old centre of Monreale, this little B&B has just a couple of elegant rooms, and it's handy for the cathedral.

€ Home from Home, *Contrada Scozzari, Bolognetta, T091-872 4848, homefromhome-sicily.com*. Owners Kathy and Toto will ensure that their guests are comfortable. Although Bolognetta is off the tourist trail, it's only 23 km from Palermo and 32 km from Corleone.

€ Portella della Ginestra, *San Giuseppe Jato, T091-857 4810, liberaterra.it*. Located near Piana degli Albanesi, 22 km south of Monreale, this estate formerly belonged to Mafia boss Bernardo Brusca; it is now run by the *Libera Terra* (Free Earth) cooperative. The B&B is set in the renovated farmhouse, and activities include horse riding and hiking. The only downside is the relative proximity of a main road.

Self-catering

€€ Masseria La Chiusa, *Contrada Chiusa, San Giuseppe Jato, T091-857 7783, masserialachiusa.com*. This *agriturismo* occupies a working farm dating back to the 15th century and is located about 20 km from Palermo. Choose from apartments (from €90 per night/€500 per week for two people; or €180 per night/€750-1000 per week for four people) or B&B accommodation in double or triple rooms (some of which have jacuzzis). It's great for families, and has a pool, children's playground, tennis court, and an excellent restaurant, and makes a good base for hiking, riding, and mountain-biking.

Sant'Agata Agriturismo, *Località Sant'Agata, SP5 Km 17.800, Piana degli Albanesi, T338-459 8654, santagataturismo.it*. Overlooking sun-baked fields of wheat 28 km south of Palermo and 9 km south of Piana degli Albanesi on the SP5 this 19th-century *masseria* has been restored. There's a pool in the gardens, and a restaurant serving the estate's own produce.

Cefalù and the Madonie *p45 and p47*

€€€ Relais Santa Anastasia, *Contrada Santa Anastasia, Castelbuono, T0921-672233, santa-anastasia-relais.it*. A luxurious rural retreat in a handsomely restored 12th-century stone abbey, whose amenities include a fabulous pool with views of the surrounding Madonie mountains, relaxing gardens and a decent restaurant. The hotel is about 30 minutes' drive from Cefalù.

€€ ART Hotel Atelier sul Mare, *Via Cesare Battisti 4, Castel di Tusa, T0921-334295, ateliersulmare.it*. Antonio Presti organized the Fiumara d'Arte, a fantastic outdoor sculpture park in Castel di Tusa, and is also behind the ART hotel. Choose between the striking artist-designed rooms, or the simpler standard rooms at a lower price. The best offer sea views, though be prepared for the sound of trains on the nearby railway line.

€€ Masseria Maggiore, *Contrada Stranghi, Pettineo, T380-545 1891 (mob), masseriamaggiore.it*. A luxury mountain hideaway, 20 minutes' drive from Cefalù, with pool, gardens and restaurant. You could hole up here in this *agriturismo* and forget the outside world for a few days, or else take to the hills and explore the stunning natural parks on foot, mountain bike or horseback. Choose from elegant suites or the small self-catering cottage (€60-115 per person per night).

€€-€ Villa Gaia, *Via V Pintorno, T0921-420992, villagaiahotel.it*. Book early for a room at this modern hotel in Cefalù, which fills up quickly thanks to its central location across the road from the beach, friendly staff and smart rooms and suites. It's worth splashing out a little extra for a balcony with sea view.

€ Dolce Vita B&B, *Via C.O. Bordonaro 8, T0921-923151, dolcevitabb.it*. This simple B&B is located up a steep flight of stairs in the heart of Cefalù's beautiful old quarter, with lovely sea views from the shared terrace and from some of the rooms.

€ Giardino Donna Lavia, *SS643, Polizzi Generosa, about 60km from Cefalù. T0921-551104, giardinodonnalavia.com*. A very friendly little *agriturismo*, this is set in a beautifully restored stone farmhouse in the Madonie with a stunning mountain backdrop. Family-run and welcoming, it offers just four simple rooms, plus a larger suite in a 13th-century watchtower. Numerous activities can be arranged, including horse riding, hiking and even skiing in nearby Piano Battaglia. The restaurant serves a set menu of traditional mountain cuisine every evening, and is open to non-guests.

€ Villa Rainò, *Contrada da Rainò, Gangi, T0921-644680, villaraino.it*. The perfect country retreat, this handsome old manor house 4 km outside Gangi in the Madonie mountains boasts simple rooms and a superb restaurant. There's a pool, with great views, and some fine walking in the surrounding hills.

Self-catering

Monaco di Mezzo, *Resuttano, near Petralia Sottana, T0934-673949, monacodimezzo.com*. At this beautiful, 18th-century farmhouse set in rolling hills 32 km south of Petralia Sottana you can choose between nine rustic bedrooms (€€), from room only to full board, and six self-catering apartments of various sizes (€510-650 per week for a two-bedroom apartment sleeping four). The farm produces its own organic olive oil, hams and cheeses, available for purchase and served in the restaurant. The *agriturismo* offers riding excursions into the marvellous Madonie natural park, or you could just laze by the pool.

Antico Feudo San Giorgio, *Contrada San Giorgio, SS120 Km 45.990, Polizzi Generosa, T0921-600690, feudosangiorgio.it*. This stunning, hilltop farm gazes out across the magnificent Madonie mountains, and is paradise for hikers and mountain bikers. Kids will love the animals (especially the donkeys), the pool and playground, and the chance to join in with the harvest. The *agriturismo* can accommodate up to 50 guests – from B&B (€) to self-catering (€650-1000 per week for an apartment sleeping four to six) – and there's a restaurant and cookery lessons on offer.

Ustica *p47*

€€ Hotel Clelia, *Via Sindaco I 29, T091-844 9039, hotelclelia.it*. A modern establishment with well-equipped bedrooms. The top-floor restaurant is one of the best on the island, and offers views to go with the seafood. They also rent out holiday apartments for €149-796 per week for a two-bed apartment.

€ Albergo Ariston, *Via della Vittoria 5, T091-844 9335, usticahotels.it*. A small inn with functional rooms offered at modest prices, particularly in the low season.

Self-catering
Agriturismo Hibiscus, *Contrada Tramontana, T091-844 9543, agriturismo hibiscus.com*. This working farm on Ustica's northern coast offers four delightful apartments, all simply but stylishly furnished. The apartments sleep two (€420-770 per week) or four (€840-1300).

Restaurants

Around Palermo *p41*
€€€-€€ Da Calogero, *Via Torre 22, Mondello, T091-684 1333. Daily 1230-1500, 1930-2230*. This restaurant has been offering seafood specialties such as *spaghetti con ricci* (sea urchin) and *insalata di polpo* (octopus salad) for almost 80 years. Pizzas served in the evenings.
€€ Antica Stazione Ferroviaria Ficuzza, *Via Vecchia Stazione, Ficuzza, T091-846 0000, anticastazione.it. Daily 1300-1500, 1930-2300*. Traditional cuisine prepared with local ingredients is the hallmark of this excellent restaurant set in an old railway station. Try pasta in a rich tomato and aubergine sauce, followed by an organic pork chop, and then finish with a delicious dessert. It also offers B&B accommodation in simple but comfortable rooms.
€ Don Ciccio, *Via del Cavaliere 87, Bagheria, T091-932442. Mon, Tue, Thu-Sat 1300-1500 and 1900-2200*. This trattoria serves Sicilian classics like *sarde a beccafico* (sardines stuffed breadcrumbs and pine nuts), pasta with tuna sauce (in early summer), and *cannoli* and *cassata*. It's near the villa Palagonia.

Cafés and bars
Il Baretto, *Viale Regina Elena, Mondello. Usually daily in summer, weekends in winter, subject to weather*. This little beachfront kiosk sells fantastic artisanal ice cream.
Pasticceria Don Gino, *Via Dante 66, Bagheria, T091-968778. Daily 0800–2100*. This smart pastry shop and café has been going for well over half a century, although you wouldn't think so from the contemporary décor. The award-winning cakes and snacks from the *tavola calda* draw Sicilians from across the island. Light meals also available.

Cefalù and the Madonie *p45 and p47*
€€€ Nangalarruni, *Via dell Confraternite 5, Castelbuono, T0921-671428, hostaria nangalarruni.it. Thu-Tue 1230-1500, 1930-2200*. This relaxed, traditional restaurant is tucked away in one of the narrow streets that make up Castelbuono's medieval core. Local dishes from the Madonie are the speciality, with succulent meat (including wild boar), wild mushrooms, velvety cheeses and charcuterie from the mountains taking pride of place on the menu. Finish up with *testa di turco*, the traditional cream-filled pastries.
€€€ Ristorante Kentia al Trappitu, *Via Ortolani di Bordonaro 96, T0921-423801, kentiaaltrappitu.it. Wed-Mon 2030-2230, open daily in summer*. This has a stunning (and much sought-after) terrace overlooking the sea. Beautifully fresh seafood is the main draw, innovatively prepared – try the shellfish salad, or the sea bass in a courgette crust. Pizzas also available. Book early to get a table on the terrace.
€€ La Brace, *Via XXV Novembre 10, T0921-423570, ristorantelabrace.com. Tue 2000-2230, Wed-Sun 1300-1500, 2000-2230, closed 15 Dec to 15 Jan*. Just off Cefalù's piazza Duomo, La Brace serves refined Sicilian cuisine in a rustic, cosy dining room, complete with wooden furnishings and exposed stone arches. House specialities include chicken and Madeira paté, roast rabbit with chestnuts, and a magnificent marinated swordfish with lemon sauce.
€€ Osteria del Duomo, *Via Seminario 5, T0921-421838, ostariadelduomo.it. Daily 1230-2300*. With a grandstand view of Cefalù's magnificent main square and the handsome cathedral, this is a popular choice with visitors. There's a well-priced tourist menu, and the food is reliably good,

classic Sicilian fare. Get there early for an outdoor table.

€ Da Salvatore, *Piazza San Michele 3, Petralia Soprana, T0921-680169. Wed-Mon 1230-1500, 1930-2200*. At this friendly trattoria and pizzeria you'll find delicious local products from the Madonie mountains, including superb cheeses (rich, milky *provola* and a creamy ricotta among them), plus a wide range of pasta dishes flavoured with wild mushrooms and local vegetables. The place is a favourite with the locals and can be packed by 1300, so get there early. Pizzas served evenings only.

€ Trattoria Itria, *Via Beato Gnoffi 8, Polizzi Generosa, T0921-688790. Thu-Tue 1230-1500, 2000-2300*. This friendly, family-run trattoria serves up delicious pizzas baked in a wood-fired oven, along with wonderful local dishes such as tagliatelle with wild mushrooms, or roast lamb. Desserts are delicious, particularly the rich *torta al formaggio* (cheesecake).

Cafés and bars

Fiasconaro, *Piazza Margherita 10, Castelbuono, T0921-677132, fiasconaro.com*. If you want to try the local speciality, *testa di turco* ('Turk's head', a traditional cake dating back to the Turkish pirate attacks in the 16th century) you'll need to order in advance. The rich, cream-filled cake is also celebrated in early December in Castelbuono's Sagre della Testa di Turco. Among other treats, you could pick up some *mannetto*, an iced cake prepared with the local manna, a natural sweetener derived from ash trees.

Pietro Serio, *Via G Giglio 29, T0921-422293*. Cefalù's best *pasticceria*, with mouthwatering cakes and pastries, including scrumptious *cannoli*, plus handmade ice cream in a range of flavours. Stand at one of the counter tables to sample them, or take away for a picnic.

Entertainment

Cefalù *p45*
Le Calette, *Porto Presidiana, lecalettediscoclub.it. Jun-Sep 2200-0300, €10 entry includes a drink*. An upmarket club and bar beautifully set right on the rocks, this is one of the most sophisticated nightlife options in Cefalù. It's part of the hotel of the same name. In summer, there are bars along the whole length of Cefalù's *lungomare* (seafront).

Festivals and events

Around Palermo *p41*
Settimana di Musica Sacra, *Monreale. Late Nov or early Dec*. A week-long programme of classical music concerts in the sublime surroundings of Monreale's cathedral (musicasacradimonreale.it).

Cefalù and the Madonie *p45 and p47*
Sherbeth Festival, *Cefalù. Early Sep*. Ice-cream lovers shouldn't miss the annual Sherbeth Festival (sherbethfestival.it), which celebrates ice cream in every imaginable flavour. Tastings, competitions and concerts.
Sagra del Cappero, *Salina. First Sun in Jun*. A festival held in honour of Salina's famous capers, which are beloved by gourmets throughout Italy.
Festa de la Madonna de la Provvidenza, *Montalbano. 24 Aug*. This traditional festival, one of the oldest in the Nebrodi, honours the town's patron saint. The wooden statue is covered with jewels and paraded through the streets.
Festa di San Bartolomeo, *Lipari. 24 Aug*. Lipari celebrates the feast day of its patron saint with a procession of the statue of the saint through the streets, and a fabulous firework show over the sea.

🛍 Shopping

Around Palermo p41
Enogastronomia Badalamenti, *Viale Galatea 55, Mondello, T091-450213.* A huge selection of cheeses, hams, cured meats and other gourmet delights, along with more than 1000 wines. It's near the beach, and perfect for picking up picnic supplies.

Cefalù and the Madonie p45 and p47
Books
La Galleria, *Via XXV Novembre 22-24, Cefalù, T0921-420211, lagalleriacefalu.it. Daily 1100-2400.* This light, bright stylish café combines bookshop, gallery, restaurant and internet café in one. There is a small selection of books in foreign languages, including a decent choice of English books. The food is fresh, tasty and modern, although rather expensive. Best of all is the lovely courtyard – an enchanting dining venue in summer.

Ceramics
Ceramiche d'Angelo, *Via Garibaldi 38, Polizzi Generosa, T0921-649173, ceramiche dangelo.it. Mon-Fri 1000-1300, 1700-1900, Sat 1000-1300.* The ceramics of the Madonie are famous. In this workshop on the edge of the old town, you'll find a range of hand-painted ceramics, from traditional tableware to contemporary decorative objects.

🎭 What to do

Around Palermo p41
Food and wine
Anna Tasca Lanza/Regaleali, *Contrada Regaleali, Sclafani Bagni, T0934-814654, annatascalanza.com, tascadalmerita.it.* Anna Tasca Lanza was born in the Villa Tasca and grew up on the vast family estate, Regaleali. Her father began the celebrated Tasca d'Almerita winery, and her cooking school is now world famous. The school is now run by Anna's daughter, Fabrizio. A lunch class costs €150, or you can spend five days on the estate for €2000.

Wellbeing
Grand Hotel delle Terme, *Piazza delle Terme 2, Termini Imerese, T091-8113557, grandhoteldelleterme.it.* Treat yourself at this luxurious 19th-century hotel, which draws on hot springs that have been famous since Roman times for their curative properties. A weekend spa package, including thermal baths and a massage, costs from €65 per person. Bed and breakfast in a double room costs €85-120 for two.

Ustica p47
There are several diving companies operating on Ustica, most open from May to October. The island is a protected nature reserve, and numerous species including barracuda, amberjack and grouper are commonly seen. Prices are fairly standard: around €40 for a single dive; €330 for a 10-dive package; or €420 for a six-day open water course. All dive companies rent out equipment. Recommended establishments include the following:

Profondo Blu Ustica, *via Cristoforo Colombo, T091-844 9609, ustica-diving.it.* Also has a good B&B.
Orca, *T334-216 1588, orcasub.it.*
Mare Nostrum Diving, *via Cristoforo Colombo, T330-792589, marenostrumdiving.it.*

🚍 Transport

Around Palermo p41
Regular AMAT (T848-800817, amat.pa.it) buses link central Palermo with **Mondello** (buses 806 and 833 from piazza Politeama, or several services from the piazzale de Gasperi by the Parco della Favorita) and **Monreale** (bus 389 from piazza Indipendenza). Tickets €1.30 if pre-purchased from bars or ticket kiosks, or onboard €1.70.

Bagheria (11 mins) and **Termini Imerese** (35 mins) are most conveniently reached by regular train services from Stazione Centrale. Both are also linked by bus with **AST** (T091-680 0011, aziendasicilianatrasporti.it).

The hills behind Palermo are most easily explored by your own transport, but there are bus services to **Corleone** (3-5 services Mon-Sat, 1 hr 30 mins), via Ficuzza (1 hr 15 mins), with AST and **Gallo** (T091-617 1141). **Presti** (T091-586351, prestiaecomande.com) operate bus services to **Piana degli Albanesi** (6 a day Mon-Sat, 45 mins) from via Balsamo.

Cefalù and the Madonie *p45 and p47*

The old centre of Cefalù is very small, and easy to get around on foot. It's largely pedestrianized, so you'll have to leave your car in the modern part of town (it's usually fairly easy to find roadside parking along the seafront via lungomare G Giardino) and make the short walk into the centre.

Local and regional bus services arrive outside the train station at the piazza Stazione, T0921-421169. The main bus companies in this region are **SAIS** (T800-211020, saisautolinee.it) and **AST** (T091-6800011, aziendasicilianatrasporti.it), which have services to Palermo and many of the inland towns of the Madonie (including Castelbuono, Gangi, and Polizzi Generosa).

The train station, **Stazione FS**, is on piazza Stazione, T0921-421169, trenitalia.it.

Ustica *p47*

Siremar (T091-582403, siremar.it) operates a ferry and hydrofoil service to Ustica from Palermo's Stazione Marittima. The ferries are slower but cheaper (2 hrs 40 mins, €15 one way) than hydrofoils (1 hr 15 mins, €20). **Siremar** also operates a summer-only ferry service between Ustica and Naples.

There is a limited local minibus service on the island (routes run clockwise and anti-clockwise). Buy tickets on board (€1).

Directory

Cefalù and the Madonie *p45 and p47*
Money There are several ATMs along corso Ruggero, in the old town, and several more along via Roma, including **Banco di Sicilia**, via Roma 139, T0921-931410.
Medical services Fondazione Istituto San Rafaele Ospedate G Giglio, Contrada Pietrapollastra, Pisciotto, T0921-920111, hsrgiglio.it. There are several pharmacies, including **Farmacia Battaglia**, via Roma 13, T0921-421789 (Mon 1600-1900, Tue-Sat 0900-1300, 1600-1900). **Post office** Via Vazzana 2, T0921-925511, poste.it (Mon-Fri 0800-1830, Sat 0800-1230). **Tourist information** AST, corso Ruggero 77, T0921-421050, comune.cefalu.pa.it. There's also an information office for the Parco delle Madonie in Cefalù: corso Ruggero 116, T0921-923327, parcodellemadonie.it, madonie.it.

Ustica *p47*
Money ATMs are on the main square, including the **Banco di Sicilia**, piazza Capitano Vito Longo 5, T091-844 9010.
Medical services First-aid surgery at **Largo Gran Guardia 1**, T091-844 9333.
Farmacia Zattoni, piazza Umberto I 30, T091-844 9382, Mon-Fri 0800-1230, 1700-1900, Sat 0800-1230.
Post office Piazza Armeria 9, T091-844 9394, poste.it (Mon-Fri 0800-1330, Sat 0800-1230). **Tourist information** There's no tourist office on the island.

Contents

56 Trapani and around
- 57 Trapani
- 57 East of Trapani
- 60 South of Trapani
- 62 Listings

65 The Egadi Islands and Pantelleria
- 66 The Egadi Islands
- 67 Pantelleria
- 68 Listings

Western Sicily

Trapani and around

Trapani is an inviting harbour town spread along a slender headland. It was founded by the Elymians as a port for Eryx, modern Erice, a magical hill town just inland. To the south stretches a delicate network of salt pans, overlooked by the tiny island of Mozia, once a powerful Carthaginian city. A dramatic cape juts north, dividing Trapani from the fishing villages cum seaside resorts of Castellammare del Golfo and San Vito Lo Capo; between them stretches the Zingaro Reserve, perhaps the most beautiful stretch of coast in Sicily. Inland, the temple of Segesta is sublimely set in a pristine valley.

Trapani → *For listings, see pages 62-64.*

Ignore the scruffy sprawl on Trapani's outskirts: the city's historic heart is a charmer. Compact and surprisingly elegant, it boasts a minuscule core of winding medieval streets, and a couple of Baroque avenues with splendid *palazzi*. Trapani's main monuments were thoroughly scrubbed up in 2005, when it hosted the trials for the prestigious America's Cup sailing competition, although the port is still gritty. For beaches, head south a few kilometres to Lido Di Maransa.

Old Town (Cenni Storici)
Corso Vittorio Emanuele is old Trapani's main street, a handsome, pedestrianized boulevard. Its eastern end is dominated by the enormous **Cattedrale di San Lorenzo** ⓘ *daily 0800-1600*, built in 1421 but entirely remodelled in the 18th century; it contains a *Crucifixion* attributed to Anton van Dyck (1599-1641). At the tip of the headland, by the squat Torre di Ligny, there are fabulous views out to the Egadi Islands. The finest Baroque church in Trapani is the **Chiesa di Maria SS del Soccorso**, better known as Badia Nuova, on via Torrearsa. Some resplendent Baroque *palazzi* and churches line via Garibaldi. The 16th-century **Palazzo Ciambra** (also known as the Torre Giudecca) is an exquisite example of the Spanish Plateresque style – it overlooks the main street of the former Jewish quarter (Giudecca). At the corner of via Garibaldi and via Torrearsa, the 19th-century **Mercato del Pesce** ⓘ *Mon-Sat 0800-1500*, is a splendid setting for Trapani's famous fish market. The sweeping via XXX Gennaio marks the eastern boundary of the old town. Just beyond it are Trapani's leafy public gardens, the 19th-century **Villa Margherita**, with an outdoor theatre and a pond.

Santuario dell'Annunziata
ⓘ *Via Conte Agostino Pepoli 178, T0923-539184. Daily 0800-1200, 1600-1900.*
Modern Trapani, otherwise bland and uninteresting, is redeemed by two monuments that stand side by side on a square 2 km east of the old centre. The Santuario dell'Annunziata contains the venerated *Madonna di Trapani*, a 14th-century statue by Nino Pisano or his school. At the Madonna's feet are a poignant heap of ex-votos from miracle-seeking parishioners.

Museo Regionale Pepoli
ⓘ *Via Conte Agostino Pepoli 200, T0923-553269. Tue-Sat 0900-1330, Sun and holidays 0900-1230, €6/3 concession, free for EU citizens, under 18 and over 65.*
Next door to the Sanctuary, a former convent is a beautiful setting for an enjoyably eclectic collection of painting, sculpture and decorative arts, including curiosities made from coral.

East of Trapani → *For listings, see pages 62-64.*

Some of Sicily's most beautiful sights are easily accessible from Trapani, including the dreamy hill town of Erice, the temple at Segesta, and the magnificent coastal nature reserve at Zingaro. There are also great beaches at San Vito Lo Capo and Castellammare del Golfo.

Erice

ⓘ *Erice has been pedestrianized and visitors must leave their cars at the main car park by the porta Trapani, for which there is a charge during Aug and early Sep. There's a free car park 400 m away, with a free shuttle bus to the porta Trapani. Erice is most easily reached via a cable car (Funivia, funiviaerice.it), which swings up from Trapani below in about 15 (hair-raising) mins. Take bus 23 from the bus station on piazza Vittorio Emanuele to terminal on via Caserta; departures daily Tue-Fri 0740-2030 and Sat-Sun 0940-2400, usually closed for a period between mid-Jan to mid-Mar for maintenance. €3.80 single, €6.50 return. Start early to enjoy the best views; cloud tends to gather later in the day.*

Erice is a perfectly preserved medieval town, literally lost in the clouds atop Monte San Guliano (750 m). It was founded by the Elymians in the seventh century BC, and has been associated with the goddess of love since the Elymians erected a temple to Venus. The huge Noman Castello di Venere, which still dominates the southeastern flank of the mountain, was built from the ruins of the once-celebrated temple. Although the tight maze of narrow alleys recalls an Arabic casbah, most of what survives today was built under the Normans and the Spanish. It's easy to get lost – but getting lost is the best way to discover Erice's secret courtyards (*cortiles*) with their flowers and fountains.

The imposing **porta Trapani** is the gateway to the pedestrianized old quarter. Behind it, overlooking a little cobbled square to the left, is the restrained Gothic **Real Duomo** ⓘ *1000-1230, 1500-1800, mornings only in winter, €3 admission to treasury*, with a graceful portal. The unusual detached bell tower, the **Torre Campanario** ⓘ *1000-1230, 1500-1800, mornings only in winter, €1.50*, is also known as the Torre di Re Federico II, and can be climbed for outstanding views.

The steep, cobbled **corso Vittorio Emanuele** is the little town's main drag, lined with cafés, souvenir shops and restaurants (don't miss Maria's famous pastry shop and café, on the left at No 14). Many of the shops display the colourful local carpets, *frazzate*, which are typical of Erice and are made of tightly woven coloured rags in geometric designs. The street opens out onto the **piazza Umberto I**, the main square with a handful of terrace cafés and the town hall, which contains the **Museo Cordici** ⓘ *Mon and Thu 0800-1400, 1430-1700, Tue-Wed, Fri 0800-1400, free*. This enjoyably old-fashioned museum has a collection of archaeological finds and a few paintings, notably Antonello Gagini's Annunciation.

Erice has several delightful squares, including the pretty **piazza San Domenico**, which is is overlooked on one side by the church of the same name and on the other by a line of handsome *palazzi*. Look out too for the Chiesa di San Pietro and its adjoining monastery: the latter contains the **Ettore Majorana Foundation and Centre of Scientific Culture** (EMFCSC) run by the physicist Antonino Zichichi. He is a well-known, if controversial, Italian media personality, famous for his insistence that science is not incompatible with religion.

There's another fine Barque church on the **piazza San Giuliano**, named after another fine Baroque church. From here, the via Roma sweeps down to Erice's beautiful public gardens, the **Giardino del Balio**, which offer breathtaking views. From the gardens, a series of steep steps lead up to the **Castello di Venere** ⓘ *0900-1700, donations requested*, the most spectacular of Erice's surviving fortifications, with more heart-stopping views from its walkways and battlements.

Castellammare del Golfo

ⓘ *53 km east of Trapani.*

Castellammare del Golfo, a pretty tumble of ochre and yellow houses clustered around a bay, forms the nucleus of a popular summer resort with long sandy beaches. The town was founded by the Elymians as a port for Segesta (see below), and its heart is still the harbour. The *tonnara* (tuna fishery), long closed, is now a smart hotel, but fishermen from the dwindling fleet still sit on the quay to mend their nets. The harbour is guarded by the squat **Castello Arabo-Normanno** ⓘ *Mon-Fri 0900-1300, 1500-1900, daily in Aug, T0924-30217*, which houses the local museum, as well as a tourist information office (open same hours as museum).

Scopello
ⓘ *8 km northwest of Castellammare del Golfo.*

Scopello is a picture-postcard village of rosy stone clustered around an 18th-century *baglio* (fortified house). It overlooks a bewitching stretch of coastline, with tiny coves dotted with rocks and islets. Its permanent population numbers only 80: in August, that can swell tenfold, and it's standing room only in the pretty *baglio* courtyard, with its popular restaurants and bars. The village is the main access point for the magnificent Riserva Naturale dello Zingaro.

Riserva Naturale dello Zingaro
ⓘ *Southern entrance at Scopello, northern entrance at San Vito Lo Capo, T0924-35108, riservazingaro.it. Apr-Sep 0700-2100, Oct-Mar 0800-1600, €3/2 concession, free under 10.*

The Zingaro nature reserve occupies the eastern part of the spectacular headland that culminates in San Vito Lo Capo, and includes 7 km of breathtakingly beautiful coastline. Inland, the scrub-covered slopes are home to a wealth of flora and fauna, including one of the last pairs of Bonelli's Eagle on Sicily. There are several wonderful hiking paths, marked on the plan obtainable at the park entrances, but the most popular is the coastal path.

San Vito Lo Capo
ⓘ *Tourist information at via Savoia 57, T0923-621211, comune.sanvitolocapo.tp.it.*

The long rocky finger that juts north beyond Trapani culminates dramatically in Monte Cofano. Beyond this crag is San Vito Lo Capo (38 km north of Trapani), a former fishing village surrounded by a modern sprawl of apartment buildings. Every summer, visitors descend in droves to colonize the fabulous white beaches – formed from tiny shells. San Vito Lo Capo is famous for its *couscous di pesce*, a celebrated North African dish given a Sicilian twist with the addition of fresh fish, which gets its own festival in September (visit couscousfest.it for more information).

Alcamo
ⓘ *55 km east of Trapani.*

Alcamo, a trim little agricultural town surrounded by snaking vines, is the capital of one of Sicily's best known winemaking regions. Some of the local vineyards accept visitors; check with the tourist office. The seaside satellite, Alcamo Marina, has more fine sandy beaches.

Segesta
ⓘ *Signposted off the A29 Palermo–Trapani autostrada, 36 km east of Trapani, 7 km west of Calatafimi, T0924-952356, 0900-1700 (ticket office closes at 1600). Entrance tickets (€6/3 concession) and bus tickets (€1.50) for the shuttle to the top of the hill are available from the café-bar and shop by the car park.*

Nothing quite prepares you for the first glimpse of Segesta. There's a crook in the country road, and suddenly the vast temple appears from the folds of the green hills like a mirage.

Little is known about the Elymians, one of the earliest peoples on Sicily, nor about the founding of Segesta, their most important city. It enters recorded history only around 500 BC, but had been founded centuries earlier. The city was destroyed by its rival Selinunte (see page 74) in 409 BC and never recovered its former power and influence. Segesta was one of the first cities to ally with the Romans, who invaded Sicily in the third century BC, and was later destroyed by Vandals. What little remained was shattered by an earthquake.

The highlight is the temple, built around 430 BC, one of the best-preserved Doric temples in the world. Curiously, there is no roof, which has given rise to a number of different theories. The most captivating of these is that the temple was only built to dazzle the Athenians, whom the Segestans wanted as allies in their war with arch-rival Selinunte. Once the Athenians left, having satisfied themselves of the wealth and taste of the Segestans, the locals didn't bother to finish it.

A steep path winds up through scrub and wild herbs to the top of the hill in 20-30 minutes, or you can take the shuttle bus from just outside the bar. Crowning the hill is a superb Greek theatre, carved into the pale stone in the third century BC, and looking out over undulating hills all the way to the coast. A festival of Greek theatre is held here every summer (end July to end August, festivalsegesta.com). The Arabs and then the Normans occupied the site briefly, and remnants of a mosque and a church are visible just beyond the theatre.

South of Trapani

Via del Sale (the Salt Route)

The silvery outline of Trapani's famous salt lagoons stretch south to Marsala, dotted with the silhouettes of wooden-sailed windmills. The SP21 – the 'Via del Sale' – is a panoramic back road that skirts the coast. Trapani salt is highly regarded as a gourmet item thanks to its rich mineral content and the traditional, chemical-free process by which it is made. There are two main areas of production: the **Saline di Trapani**, around the hamlet of Nubia about 6 km south of Trapani, and the hauntingly beautiful **Stagnone di Marsala**, 20 km south of Trapani, a vast lagoon dotted with islands, which is a protected nature reserve.

In the coastal hamlet of **Nubia**, a picturesque windmill contains the **Museo del Sale** ⓘ *via delle Saline, T0923-867442*, where you can learn about the history of salt-making. It sits on the edge of the **Riserva Saline di Trapani e Paceco** ⓘ *visitor centre, Mulino Maria Stella, via Garibaldi 138, Contrada Nubia, T0923-867700, wwfsalineditrapani.it, free guided visits in Italian on Fri*, a WWF-run Mecca for birdwatchers.

The southern salt pans fringe the edge of the **Stagnone di Marsala**, the largest lagoon in Sicily, which averages just 1 m in depth, now a nature reserve. By the water's edge (follow signs for the Saline Ettore e Infersa) there's another restored (and functioning) **windmill** ⓘ *Contrada Ettore Infersa, T0923-733003, 0900-1300, 1500 till dusk, €3*. It overlooks the slip for boats to the Isola di San Pantoleo, which is more commonly known as Mozia for the important Phoencian settlement of Motya (see below) which once occupied the island.

Mozia (Isola di San Pantoleo)

ⓘ *Follow signs for Imbarcadero Saline Infersa off the SP21 to reach the jetty, T0923-989249. Boats €6 return, summer 0900-1330, 1430-1900, winter 0900-1600.*

It's hard to believe that great swathes of the Mediterranean were controlled from this little island, but ancient Motya was once a powerful city state. It was founded during the eighth century BC by the Phoenicians, but reached the peak of its power under the Carthaginians during the fifth and fourth centuries BC. In 397 BC it was razed after a siege by Dionysos I, tyrant of Syracuse, who slaughtered every inhabitant. It was recaptured a year later, but never regained its former influence. For the last 2000 years or more, it has been home only to a handful of fishermen, apart from a brief period during the 11th century when Basilian monks established a small community and dedicated the island to San Pantoleo.

The island has been owned by the Whitakers (the British family who made a fortune through Marsala wine) since Joseph 'Pip' Whitaker, an enthusiastic amateur archaeologist, heard that some unusual finds had been discovered by locals. He uncovered one of the best preserved Phoenician sites anywhere in the Mediterranean. Some remarkable finds are on display in the small **Museo Whitaker** ⓘ *summer 0900-1245, 1400-1900, winter 0900-1245, 1500-1800, T0923-712598, €9/5 concession*, which now occupies the lovely, tree-shaded villa. Pride of place goes to the celebrated fifth-century BC statue, **Il Giovane di Motia**, of a young man with confident pose and beautifully rendered garments, one of the finest pieces of Greek sculpture in Sicily. There are lots of finds from the Tophet burial ground, including urns which contained the ashes of sacrificed animals or cremated children (opinion is divided on whether the Phoenicians sacrificed children to their gods, or whether these are the remains of children who died naturally), and grinning masks placed in burial sites to ward off evil spirits.

Outside the villa, look for the **Casa dei Mosaici**, with faded designs picked out in black and white stones. A pathway makes a loop around the island, passing the ancient **Kothon** (port) and dry dock, and the underwater vestiges of the Roman-built causeway that once linked the city to the mainland (and was in use right up until 1971).

Trapani and around listings

For hotel and restaurant price codes and other relevant information, see pages 11-16.

Where to stay

Trapani and around p56

€€ La Gancia, *Piazza Mercato del Pesce, Trapani, T0923-438060, lagancia.com.* This comfortable aparthotel offers elegantly decorated suites, the best of which boast superb sea views. The suites can be booked on a nightly B&B basis, or, if you want to stay longer (minimum four nights), as self-catering units (all come equipped with small kitchenettes).

€€-€ Hotel Cetarium, *Via Don Leonardo Zangara 45, Castellammare del Golfo, T0924-533401, hotelcetarium.it.* Sitting right on the piquant little port, with views over the working fishing boats and yachts, this former *tonnara* has been converted into a stylish hotel. Rooms are small but comfortable, with contemporary furnishings, and there's a restaurant and fashionable bar.

€ Ai Lumi, *Corso Vittorio Emanuele 71, T0923-872418, ailumi.it.* A lovely *palazzo* on Trapani's elegant (pedestrianized) main street houses this appealing B&B, with rooms distributed around a patio. There's a restaurant downstairs (see below), where guests are given a 15% discount. Simple self-catering apartments are also available.

€ Almaran B&B, *Via S Cristoforo 8, T0923-549847, almaran.it.* A very friendly little B&B in the old quarter of Trapani, this offers a handful of simple rooms at a bargain price. Rooms are bright and spotless, all boasting private bathrooms and air conditioning, and the owner is full of great tips.

€ Baglio la Luna, *Riserva dello Zingaro, San Vito Lo Capo, T335-836 2856, bagliolaluna. com. Open Apr-Nov.* On the edge of the Zingaro Reserve, this B&B enjoys a breathtaking location high above the sea. There are three pretty rooms, a fabulous garden with a play area, and a magnificent terrace. It's worth paying the small supplement for a room with a sea view.

€ L'Antica Cascina del Golfo, *Contrada Scopello 101, Scopello, T 339-1005668, anticacascinadelgolfo.com.* This delightful little B&B occupies an eyrie-like position above the bay, and commands stunning views out across the coastline from the terrace. The rooms are pretty, the owners friendly, and breakfasts include wonderful homemade cakes and pastries.

Self-catering

Le Chiavi di San Francesco Hotel, *Via Tartaglia 18-20, T0923-438013, lechiavidisanfrancesco.com.* This smart apart-hotel is tucked away in a converted *palazzo* in the heart of Trapani's old centre (although the original interior has been replaced with modern furnishings). It offers attractively, if simply, furnished apartments for two to four people with basic kitchenettes (€80-160/€90-200 per night respectively). Breakfast is served on a panoramic roof terrace, with wonderful views over the old town with its spires and domes.

Tarantola, *Contrada Tarantola, Alcamo, T329-271 3073, gorgodeldrago.it.* Set amid a sea of vines, this tranquil *agriturismo* and working wine estate offers accommodation in attractively refurbished outbuildings. Choose from B&B (€70-100) or one of the self-catering apartments (€120-200, sleeps 4). Their own produce is used in the restaurant.

Restaurants

Trapani and around p56

€€€ Dal Cozzaro, *Via Savoia 15, San Vito Lo Capo, T0923-972777, dalcozzaro.it. Daily 1230-1530, 1900-2330.* A long-established classic, this buzzy restaurant serves a wide range of couscous dishes (served with vegetables, meat or fish), plus wonderfully fresh fish of the day, and excellent salads. Prices are moderate, and good value for the quality on offer.

€€€ Ristorante del Golfo, *Via Segesta 153, Castellamare del Golfo, T0924-30257. Wed-Mon 1230-1500, 1930-2200. Closed 2 weeks in Oct.* Book early for a table at this minuscule but well regarded restaurant, where you will be served whatever came in on the fishing boats that morning. Fresh seafood is prepared to traditional recipes.

€€ Ai Lumi, *Corso Vittorio Emanuele 71, Trapani. T0923 872418, ailumi.it. Mon-Sat 1900-2300, Aug daily. Closed Nov.* Rustic wooden tables and checked tablecloths belie the sophistication of this Trapani *tavernetta*, which serves some of the best food in town. Start with antipasti and home-made bread, and follow up with grilled fish. They also run a charming B&B.

€€ Cantina Siciliana, *Via Giudecca 32, Trapani, T0923-28673, cantinasiciliana. it. Daily 1230-1500, 1930-2200.* A long-established and atmospheric *trattoria* in Trapani's old Jewish quarter, this serves market-fresh cuisine like *rotolini gamberetti e uovo di tonno* – a pasta pocket stuffed with tiny shrimp, hazelnuts and tuna roe. Order *cassatelle* (fried pastry parcels with ricotta and cinnamon) for dessert.

€€ Massimo, *Porta Trapani, Erice, T0923-869692, massimoristorante.it.* The tasty local specialities here include a wonderful risotto with prawns and almonds and steak cooked in Marsala wine. Book a table on the terrace to enjoy romantic views.

€€ Monte San Giuliano, *Vicolo San Rocco 7, Erice, T0923-869595. Mon-Sat 1300-1500, 1900-2200. Closed 3 weeks in Jan and 3 weeks in Nov.* Tucked away in Erice's beautiful stone heart, this pretty restaurant is a great place to try *cuscus di pesce* (fish couscous) or a wide range of flavoursome, home-made pasta dishes. Book a table on the plant-shaded terrace.

€€ Versi di Rosso, *Corso Vittorio Emanuele 63, Trapani, T334-627 3949. Daily 1900–2400.* A stylish *enoteca* on the old town's main drag, with a carefully selected wine list and a menu packed with delicious local specialities. The seafood couscous is excellent. Book in advance. Highly recommended.

Cafés and bars

Il Gelato di Michele, *Viale Regina Margherita 25, Trapani, T0923-873942. Daily 0900-1900, weekends only in winter.* If you can't make up your mind which flavour to choose, go for the intense dark chocolate.

Minaudo, *Via Gioacchino Amico 12, San Vito Lo Capo, T0923-972549. Daily 1100-2100. Closed in winter.* Widely considered the best *gelateria* in town, with a huge range of flavours to choose from. Try the fantastic *granita di arance rosse*, made with blood oranges.

Pane Cunzato, *Scopello.* This simple bakery tucked down a side street from the main square is renowned for its eponymous 'pane cunzato' sandwiches (cheese, tomato, oregano and, occasionally, anchovies, layered onto a fresh ciabatta-style loaf drizzled with olive oil). You can eat out on the tables in the courtyard.

⚘ Festivals and events

Trapani and around *p56*
I Misteri di Trapani. Trapani's Easter processions are the most famous in Sicily. A series of floats topped with scenes from the Passion of Christ (the events leading up to the Crucifixion) are processed through crowd-lined streets on Good Friday and Holy Saturday. Even if you're not here at Easter you can see the figures in the little **Chiesa del Purgatorio** (via San Francesco d'Assisi, daily 1600-1830), which is murky with incense.

Luglio Musicale Trapanese, *Trapani. Jul.* Opera festival held at the Villa Margherita public gardens. See lugliomusicale.it.

Zampogna d'Oro, *Erice. Early Dec.* Folklore music festival.

🛍 Shopping

Trapani and around *p56*
Pasticceria Maria Grammatico, *Corso Vittorio Emanuele 14, Erice, T0923-869390, mariagrammatico.it. Daily 0800-2100.* A superb pastry shop (and café), which is famous throughout Sicily. Maria's story is told in *Bitter Almonds* by Mary Taylor Simeti.
Renda, *Via Giovanbattista Fardella 82, Trapani, T0923-22270, renda.it. Mon-Sat 0900-1300, 1630-2000.* This deli has all kinds of local specialities, including olive oils, wines, jars of Trapanese pesto, plus cheeses, hams, salami and everything you need for a picnic.

⏰ What to do

Trapani and around *p56*
Diving
Cetaria Diving, *Via Marco Polo 3, Scopello, T368-386 4808, cetaria.com.* Diving and snorkelling in the protected Zingaro nature reserve. A half-day boat excursion with stops for snorkelling and swimming costs from around €50.

Food and wine
Fazio, *Via Capitano Rizzo 39, Fulgatore (near Erice), T0923-811700, faziowines.it.* You can arrange visits (by prior appointment) to this award-winning winery.

⊖ Transport

Trapani and around *p56*
The centre of Trapani is tiny and easy to get around on foot; a free shuttle bus runs from the train station to the sanctuary and adjoining art museum. Local buses are run by ATM (T0923-559575, atmtrapani.it). The main bus station is on via Ilio; follow signs for the 'City Terminal' or 'Autostazione'. Bus No 23 takes you to the start of the cable car for Erice.

The train station is in the centre of town at piazza Umberto I, T0923-540416.
Trapani is linked by train to Palermo (2½ hrs, 4 daily), Castellammare del Golfo (45 mins, 4 daily), Segesta-Tempio for Segesta (25 mins, 4 daily). There are at least 8 trains a day to Marsala (30 mins), and to Mazara del Vallo (50 mins). For Erice, take the cable car, or the regular AST bus (40 mins). There are infrequent trains to Salemi-Gibellina station (1½ hrs). For Mozia (Motya), take the bus or train to Marsala, and then take a local bus from there. **AST buses** (aziendasicilianatrasporti.it) link Trapani with San Vito Lo Capo (1 hr 20 mins hrs, at least 8 daily except Sun), as well as Marsala (30 mins, regular weekday services, limited at weekends), Mazara del Vallo (2½ hrs, 3 services daily), Castellammare del Golfo (1 hr) and the airport at Trapani-Birgi (also known as Vincenzo Florio airport). AST, Tarantola and Segesta buses connect Trapani with Segesta (45 mins); Segesta buses continue to Palermo (2½ hrs). Russo (T0924-31364, russoautoservizi.it) buses link Castellammare del Golfo with Scopello and San Vito Lo Capo.

ℹ Directory

Trapani *p57*
Money There are several banks along corso Italia and via Garibaldi, including **Banco di Sicilia**, via Garibaldi Giuseppe 9, T0923-821111. **Medical services Azienda Unità Sanitaria**, via Staiti, T0923-543011. **Farmacia Marini Sofia Maria**, corso Vittorio Emanuele 117, T0923-21204 (Mon-Sat 0900-1300, 1630-1930). **Post office** Piazza Vittorio Veneto 11, T0923-872016, Mon-Sat 0800-1830. **Tourist information** Piazza Saturno, T0923-544533, comune.trapani.it, comune.trapani.it/turismo, trapaniwelcome.it; also in the City Terminal bus station.

The Egadi Islands and Pantelleria

The unspoilt Egadi Islands of Favignana, Levanza and Marettimo sit just off the western coast of Sicily. Favignana, the largest and closest (just 17 km from Trapani), is the busiest, but little Levanzo and Marettimo remain refreshingly unhurried. All offer the essentials for an idyllic holiday – endless sunshine, crystal-clear waters, and a relaxed pace of life. There are no beaches, but the rocky coves are perfect for swimming and diving. Fishing is still an important industry, and ancient methods have been preserved, including the annual *Mattanza* (tuna slaughter).

Pantelleria, a volcanic island 100 km from the Sicilian mainland, is sometimes called the 'black pearl of the Mediterranean', and is famous for its celebrity visitors (Madonna, Sting and Giorgio Armani among them) and its exquisite dessert wines.

The Egadi Islands → *For listings, see pages 68-70.*

Favignana

The most accessible of the Egadi Islands, Favignana is just 17 km from the coast of mainland Sicily. Commonly described as shaped like a butterfly, one 'wing' is largely flat, the other forested, while the centre is dominated by the great hump of the Montagna Grossa (315 m). On weekends, the ferries do brisk business, depositing an endless stream of Sicilian families who come for long lunches at the island's restaurants or elaborate picnics in the beautiful rocky coves.

The main town, **Favignana Città**, is a sea of white and ochre buildings spread around the port at the centre of the 'butterfly'. The vast Florio *tonnara*, once the largest tuna-processing factory in Sicily, sits on the water's edge, and is currently being elegantly (and expensively) restored into a cultural centre. The rosy Palazzo Florio (1874), built for the scions of the dynasty that once owned the Egadis, is now part of the town hall. Piazza Matrice is the heart of the *città*, and the focus of the evening *passeggiata*. Café terraces spill their tables out onto the square, which is overlooked by the simple façade of the Chiesa Madre. The shabby fortress that stands on the hill above the town was built by the Arabs, and later expanded by the Bourbons to contain a prison – a function it fulfilled until 1860. Until recently it was used by the Italian military, but is now abandoned. The rest of the island is pocked with the scars of tufa quarries, which etch the cliff with geometrical patterns around the stunning **Cala Rossa** (in the north of the island). This is now Favignana's most beautiful bay, but got its name, according to legend, after the seas turned red with blood during the final naval battle of the First Punic War in 241 BC. There is some excellent diving around this cape. The best swimming cove is the breathtaking **Cala Azzurra** at the southeastern tip.

Levanzo

Levanzo, the smallest of the Egadi islands, lying 15 km from Trapani, is an empty, arid outcrop with a rocky coastline overlooking a cobalt sea. The only village, which overlooks the tiny port at Cala Dogana, is a simple straggle of white houses at the foot of a tall crag. There is just one road, but a series of wonderful footpaths criss-cross the island. One of the best of these leads to the celebrated **Grotto del Genovese** ⓘ *locked after vandal attacks; organize tours at least a day in advance through the custodian, T0923-924032/T339-741 8800, grottadelgenovese.it; from €15 per person, including return journey by boat or jeep*, which contains some extraordinary prehistoric paintings, discovered only by accident in 1949. Some date back to the Upper Palaeolithic era (around 10,000 BC), while the incised drawings were probably executed around 8000 BC during the Neolithic era. The paintings, among the earliest cave paintings in Italy, depict fishermen (chasing tuna, even then), farmers, and wonderful dancing figures. This is just one of numerous caves that riddle the island, many of which are only accessible by boat. It's a paradise for divers, and there have been several important submarine finds dating back to the time of the Punic wars between the Romans and the Carthaginians. Fishing remains an important industry, and the fishermen of Levanzo also participate in the annual *Mattanza*.

Marettimo

The greenest and most remote of the Egadis (24 km from Trapani), Marettimo is a rugged island paradise. Accommodation is limited, and should be booked well in advance during the peak summer season, but even then this deliciously uncommercialized spot is rarely overwhelmed. The island is a protected nature reserve, and there are some superb hikes. One of the best leads to the remnants of a fortress (which served as a prison until the mid-19th century) right at the top of Punta Troia, with wonderful views. Fishermen offer boat trips to some of the loveliest coves, many of which are only accessible by boat; ask around at the harbour, or at your accommodation.

Pantelleria → *For listings, see pages 68-70.*

The chic little celeb haunt of Pantelleria is a small volcanic island closer to Africa than to Sicily (the Tunisian coast is just 70 km away, while Marsala is 100 km in the opposite direction). It's the largest of Sicily's offshore islands (83 sq km), and preserves a strong Arabic influence, not just in the place names – Khamma, Gadir, and Bukkuram – but also in the low, domed buildings of stone called *dammusi* that dot the countryside. Vineyards planted largely with the Zibibbo grape (the Sicilian name for the Muscat of Alexandria) produce the lusciously sweet moscato and passito dessert wines (see page 69 for details of wineries offering tours), and the tangy Pantelleria capers are a delicacy beloved by gourmets.

The island was heavily bombed during the Second World War, and the main town, **Pantelleria**, is modern and scruffy. Piled up higgledy-piggledy around the harbour, it's not particularly pretty, but the narrow streets are appealingly lively, especially in summer. There are more picturesque hamlets at **Scauri**, **Nikà** and **Gadir**, which all boast harbours with volcanic springs (the latter is home to Giorgio Armani's lavish summer home). Out at the tip of the panoramic headland (the **Punto dell'Arco**) is a spectacular natural arch of putty-coloured lava that resembles the head of an elephant (the **Arco dell'Elefante**). Inland, the **Montagna Grande**, the island's highest peak at 836 m, is part of a protected nature reserve, and a beautiful region to hike. During the migrating seasons, the island attracts numerous bird species including flamingos, herons and avocets. On its northeastern flank is a volcanic lake known as **Lo Specchio di Venere** (Venus' Looking Glass) where the goddess of love apparently once admired herself and which is fed by thermal springs. The stunning coastline, with its glittering black rocks and secret coves, is perfect for submarine exploration and there are several diving companies on the island.

The Egadi Islands and Pantelleria listings

For hotel and restaurant price codes and other relevant information, see pages 11-16.

Where to stay

Egadi Islands and Pantelleria *p65*
€€€ Casa dell'Arancio, *Via Cristoforo Colombo 14, Favignana, T0923 921008, lacasadellarancio.it*. Six gorgeous rooms in an old house, with the perfect mix of contemporary style and orginal details (such as vaulted ceilings and carved antique doors). Homemade cakes are among the goodies served for breakfast. Prices from €120 (double room in low season) to €240 (suite in high season).
€€ Casa di Gloria B&B, *Contrada Penna, T328-277 0934, Pantelleria, dammusidigloria.it*. This relaxed and stylish B&B on chic Pantelleria is run by a wonderful couple, Gloria and Saura, who want every guest to feel at home. Rooms are located in a collection of beautiful *dammusi* set around a pool.
€€ Giardino di Pantelleria, *Contrada Bukkuram, Pantelleria, giardinidipantelleria.com*. A series of simple but beautifully restored *dammusi* submerged in greenery and wild flowers, this is a very romantic spot. Amenties are basic, but the views – even at night, when the owner will lend you a telescope for star-gazing – are unsurpassable. Price of a *dammusi* for two people for one week €560–1120, three people €735–1260 and four people €840–1400.
€€-€ Albergo Egadi, *Via Cristoforo Colombo 17, Favigana, T0923-921232, albergoegadi.it. Open Mar-Oct*. Just 50 m from the sea, this little inn has oodles of style. Bed and breakfast starts at €60 per person in the low season, but prices double in August. The rooms are set above a restaurant serving excellent Mediterranean cuisine.

Self-catering
Marettimo Residence, *Via Telegrafo, Marettimo, T0923-923202, marettimoresidence.com*. This offers pristine, well-equipped apartments decorated in Mediterranean blue and white (sleeping two to six people, €75-130 in low season, €115-290 in August). The apartments are distributed in low, whitewashed bungalows overlooking the sea, each with an olive-shaded terrace.
€€ Santa Teresa, *Contrada Monastero Alto, Scauri Siculo, Pantelleria, T0923-916389, santateresa.it*. This is a stunningly stylish *agriturismo* in the Monastero valley in the centre of Pantelleria. The elegantly restored *dammusi* of traditional stone are set within vineyards, olive groves and orchards.

Restaurants

Egadi Islands and Pantelleria *p65*
€€€ La Nicchia, *Via Messina 22, Pantelleria town, T0923-912968, lanicchia.it. Daily 1900-2200 in summer. Closed Oct to Easter*. One of the island's most fashionable restaurants, set in a beautifully restored *dammuso* overlooking a delightful garden. Nearby, the owners have opened a simple *enoteca*, La Nicchia sul Mare, serving a wonderful range of wines accompanied by tapas-style treats.
€€€ Paradiso, *Via Lungomare 8, Levanzo, T0923-924080, isoladilevanzo.it. Daily 1230-1500, 1900-2300. Closed mid-Nov to mid-Mar*. This classic seaside restaurant doesn't look up to much but has long been considered the best on the island. Unsurprisingly, fish predominates on the menu, with *linguine con polpo* (linguine with octopus), and fresh tuna during the Mattanza season.
€€ Il Veliero, *Via Umberto 22, Marettimo, T0923-923142. Daily 1200-1500, 1900-2200*. On the water's edge, this traditional, family-run trattoria is the best place to fill up on big plates of home cooking. Try the *busiati*

(a plump, long pasta typical of western Sicily) with a tuna sauce if it's on the menu.
€€ La Bettola, *Via Nicotera 47, Favignana, T0923-921988, isoleegadi.it/labettola. php. Fri-Wed 1230-1500, 1900-2300, daily in Aug.* A good, old-fashioned trattoria serving fresh seafood (try the lobster salad), excellent couscous, and fabulous home-made desserts.

€€ Donne Fugate, *Corso Umberto 10, Pantelleria town, T0923-912688. Daily 1200-1500, 1900-2200.* A charming little restaurant serving tasty local cuisine. The antipasti is especially recommended, particularly the carpaccio of aubergine with *bottarga* (dried tuna roe), as well as the *cuscus di pesce* (Thu only).

€ Scaletta, *Via Telegrafo 2, Marettimo, T0923-923233. Daily 0900-2200.* This manages to combine a little of everything – *pasticceria*, bar, café and an excellent, informal restaurant. Come for breakfast, a seafood lunch, or just ice cream.

Cafés and bars
Due Colonne, *Piazza Madrice 76, Favignana, T0923-922291. Daily 0800-2200.* Grab a fruit *granita* or ice cream, and watch the world go by. Also a restaurant.

Entertainment

Pantelleria *p67*
Oxidiana, *Contrada Kuddie Rosse, Pantelleria, T0923-912319.* A summer-only *discoteca* for dancing under the stars.

Festivals and events

Egadi Islands *p66*
Every year, from late April to early June, the waters turn red around the island of Favignana during the annual **Mattanza** (tuna slaughter). Using an ancient method, introduced by the Arabs and largely unchanged, the bluefin tuna are guided into a series of netted chambers, culminating in the *camera della morte*. Once the tuna are trapped in this final chamber, they are stabbed by the waiting fishermen (the *tonnaroti*) and hauled on to the boats. The sight has become a tourist attraction in recent years, and boat tours and underwater diving excursions are organized (ask at the tourist office for details).

Shopping

Pantelleria *p67*
Ceramiche de Simone, *Via Borgo Italia, T0923 913129, ceramichedesimone.com.* Brightly painted Sicilian ceramics, with bold designs inspired by Picasso, Klee and Sicilian folk art.

What to do

Pantelleria *p67*
Diving
Diving Cava Levante, *Pantelleria, T0923-915174, calalevante.it.* A reliable PADI dive centre, which offers a range of courses, including an underwater archaeology course (from €220). A single dive is €40.

Food and wine
Cantina Casano, *Contrada Kamma, Pantelleria, T0923-999314, casanovini.it.* This wine producer, famous for its Marsala wines, also produces Zibibbo wines on Pantelleria.
Salvatore Murana, *Contrada Khamma 276, Pantelleria, T0923-969673, salvatoremurana.com.* Produces superb Pantelleria wines. Tours offered.

Transport

Egadi Islands and Pantelleria *p65*
Ferries and hydrofoils link the Egadi Islands with Trapani and Marsala. **Siremar** (siremar.it) runs daily car ferry services to Favignana (45 mins) all year round. **Ustica** (usticalines.it) runs a ferry service from Marsala to the

Egadi Islands, and another from Mazara del Vallo to Pantelleria. Siremar and Ustica lines run faster hydrofoils to all three islands during the summer season (Favignana, 20 mins; Levanzo, 20 mins; Marettimo, 1 hr), and to Pantelleria (ferry 7 hrs, hydrofoil 2½ hrs). Pantelleria can also be reached by air: **Meridiana** (meridiana.it) fly daily from Trapani and Palermo during the summer, and **AirOne** (flyairone.com) operates flights from Palermo.

The easiest way to get around Pantelleria is to rent a scooter, but there is also a daily local bus service which links all the main villages. Timetables are available at comunepantelleria.it.

Directory

Favignana *p66*
Money Banco di Sicilia, piazza Madrice 12-14, T0923-921347. **Medical services** The nearest hospitals are in Trapani and Marsala. **Farmacia Barone Ilaria**, piazza Madrice 70, T0923-921265 (Mon-Fri 0900-1300, 1700-1900, Sat 0900-1300). **Post office** Via S Simone 2, T0923-923086 (Mon-Fri 0800-1330, Sat 0800-1230). **Tourist information** Pro Loco di Favignana, piazza Madrice 8, T0923-921647, turismo.trapani.it.

Contents

72 Marsala and around
- 73 Marsala
- 74 Around Marsala
- 77 Listings

80 Agrigento and around
- 81 Agrigento
- 83 Around Agrigento
- 86 Listings

Footprint features

84 Five of the best beaches

Southwestern Sicily

Marsala and around

Sicily's southwestern corner gazes out across the Strait of Sicily to Africa, and is still deeply imbued with a North African influence. Marsala owes its modern name to ninth-century Arabic rulers, and its recent prosperity to the eponymous dessert wine, popularized during the 19th century. The Arabic influence is strongest in Mazaro del Vallo, a vibrant harbour town that shelters one of Italy's largest fishing fleets. East of Mazaro del Vallo is Selinunte, another of Sicily's sublimely beautiful ancient sites. Inland, a string of interesting country towns are scattered across the Val de Belice.

Marsala → *For listings, see pages 77-79.*

Marsala is an appealing port town, slightly frayed at the edges, but still lively and even occasionally elegant. During the 19th century Marsala was famous around the globe for its amber dessert wine popularized by enterprising British businesses, the profits of which paid for the construction of lavish stile-Liberty villas which still dot the area.

Centro storico
Marsala's grandest square in the old centre is the **piazza Repubblica**, overlooked by the 18th-century **Palazzo Comunale** (city hall) and the lavish **Duomo** ⓘ *daily 1000-1200, 1500-1800*, which is dedicated to San Tommaso di Canterbury (Thomas à Becket). The frilly façade was only completed in 1956, thanks to a donation from a returning emigrant; inside there are several fine artworks including a *Madonna del Popolo* (1490) by Domenico Gagini. A lively **fish market** takes place behind the city hall every morning except Sunday.

Museo con gli Arazzi Fiamminghi
ⓘ *Via G Garaffa 57, T0923-711327. Tue-Sat 0900-1300, 1600-1800, Sun 0900-1300, €2.50.*
Behind the cathedral, this small museum contains eight exceptional 16th-century Flemish tapestries depicting scenes from the Jewish revolt against the Roman Empire (AD 66-70). They were presented to Antonio Lombardo (1523-1595), Archbishop of Messina, who is buried in the cathedral. Lombardo, who was born in Marsala, was an ambassador to Spain, where he was given the tapestries by King Felipe II.

Complesso San Pietro – Museo Garibaldino
ⓘ *Via Ludovico Anselmi Correale, T0923-718741. Tue-Sun 0900-1300, 1600-2000, €2.*
Marsala entered the history books in 1860 when Garibaldi landed here with his famous **Spedizione dei Mille** (Expedition of a Thousand) in one of the culminating episodes of the Risorgimento. Marsala's municipal museum is dedicated to the event.

Museo Archeologico Baglio Anselmi
ⓘ *Via Capo Lilibeo, T0923-952535. Tue-Sat 0900-1900 last entry 1800, Sun 0900-1300, €4/2.*
Marsala was founded by the Phoenicians after the destruction of Motya with the sonorous name of Lilybeo. It became the most important Carthaginian stronghold on Sicily, before falling to the Romans during the First Punic War. The museum, located in a wine warehouse on the seafront contains finds from ancient Lilybeo, but the highlight is the Punic warship discovered in the Stagnone lagoon. It went down around the time of the Battle of the Egadi Islands, which concluded the First Punic War in 241 BC, and was recovered in 1971. Other highlights include a pair of Roman mosaics, some gold jewellery, and the *Venus of Marsala*, a battered statue of the goddess of love (a Roman copy of a Greek original) which was mutilated by Christians.

Chiesa di San Giovanni and the Grotto of the Sibyl
ⓘ *Usually closed – ask at the tourist office.*
This 16th-century church was built over the remnants of a cave with a natural spring where the famed Sibyl of Lilybeo dwelt in ancient times. Her accuracy as a seer was renowned, but the practice of consulting oracles dwindled after the arrival of the Romans.

However, the faithful still visit the church on 24 June, feast day of San Giovanni, to ask the Sibyl to grant them luck and good fortune.

Around Marsala → *For listings, see pages 77-79.*

Mazara del Vallo, a busy harbour town with a huge fishing fleet, has a pretty if battered core, and a reminder of its ancient importance under the Arabs in the redolent Casbah. East of Mazaro del Vallo is ancient Selinunte, where the bones of temples are submerged in scrub. Inland, the beautiful Val di Belice, although devastated by an earthquake in 1968, is still dotted with sleepy country towns like Salemi and Santa Margherita.

Mazara del Vallo
ⓘ *23 km southeast of Marsala.*
One of the oldest settlements in Sicily, Mazara del Vallo is a cheerful town with a busy port, a palm-lined *lungomare*, and a small historic kernel. Just an archway survives of the Norman castle where the Sicilian parliament was called for the first time in 1097, but the 11th-century cathedral, rebuilt in the 17th century, still dominates the old town.

Mazara was founded as a trading post by the Phoenicians in the ninth century BC, but it reached the peak of its influence under the Arabs, who landed here in AD 827. Mazara quickly became one of the wealthiest cities on the island, but lost its status after the arrival of the Normans in the 11th century. Now, the Arabs are back. In the northern section of the old centre, Arabic and French are more likely to be heard than Italian, and Halal butchers and tea shops line the streets.

Most of the North African community work on the trawlers: Mazara shelters one of Italy's largest fishing fleets (although business is down as it gets harder to recruit fishermen). It was a local fisherman who landed Mazara's greatest claim to fame: the *Satiro Danzante* (*Dancing Satyr*), a bronze statue found tangled in nets in 1998. The figure, probably dates from the third or second century BC, and is exhibited at the excellent **Museo del Satiro** (in the Chiesa di Sant'Egidio) ⓘ *piazza Plebiscito, T0923-933917, Tue-Sun 0900-1800, €6.50,* where a visit includes an entertaining short film with footage of the exultant fisherman who found the statue.

Selinunte
ⓘ *Via Selinunte, Marinella di Selinunte, T0924-46540. Daily 0900-1700 (last entry 1600), summer open until 1900 (last entry 1800), €6/3 concession. See opposite for more information.*
Wild, beautiful Selinunte is curved around a quiet bay, once the colony's port. The vast ruins of a large temple dominate one hillside, while the remnants of the acropolis are strewn across another. The name comes from *selinon*, the Greek word for wild celery, which is still abundant.

Selinunte was founded in the seventh century BC by settlers from Megara Hyblaea and reached the height of its influence in the fifth century BC. Selinunte wanted to expand north and access the gulf of Castellammare but the Elymian city of Segesta stood in its path. This rivalry would lead to the destruction of Selinunte by the Carthaginians, allies of Segesta, in 409 BC. Selinunte would never fully recover. It supported Syracuse against the Carthaginians at the end of the fourth century BC, but finally submitted to Carthage in 276 BC. Only 25 years later, the city was evacuated and its people sent to Lilybeo (see Marsala, above). Selinunte was abandoned, although there were small settlements during the Arab and Norman occupations.

East Hill The most immediately impressive ruins are those of the East Hill temples, which are usually referred to by letters as their dedication is still uncertain. There are three temples in the group, of which the most complete is **Temple E** (closest to the visitor centre). Some of its exquisitely carved *metopes* can be seen in Palermo's archaeological museum (see page 33). Beyond it are the sparse remnants of **Temple F**, which was the oldest of the trio, reduced now to little more than a tumble of overgrown stones. A splendid line of huge columns are all that remains of **Temple G**, which would once have been one of the largest and most imposing temples of antiquity.

Acropolis A path winds down the valley from the temples, skipping over brooks, to emerge at the road which leads to the second area of excavations, the acropolis. This is the real heart of the city, where the people of Selinunte lived, worked and prayed. It is thought a population of around 20,000 lived within the ancient walls. The ruins are beautifully set overlooking the sea, but are very sparse: it is possible to make out the two main thoroughfares, one running north-south, the other east-west, but of the five temples that once stood within the city walls, only **Temple C** can be discerned.

Sanctuary West of the acropolis, the third set of excavations occupy a gentle hill above a second bay which would also have served as a port. Very little survives of the **Sanctuary of Demeter Malophoros** (Malophoros means 'pomegranate-bearer', and refers to a fertility goddess), which was built on the route to the necropolis, so that the bereaved could pray to the earth mother goddess, deity of life and death.

Selinunte essentials Signposted off the SP56, 2 km east of Marinella di Selinunte, 22 km south of Mazara el Vallo. Local AST and Marinella buses link Mazara del Vallo with Marinella di Selinunte, and stop at the site entrance.

The excavations are laid out in three main areas: the temples on the Collina Orientale (East Hill), closest to the visitor centre; the Acropoli (Acropolis), across the bay; and the Santuario di Demetra Malophoros (Sanctuary of Demeter Malophorus), beyond the acropolis, across the dry bed of the Modione River. See above for details. The unofficial website selinunte.net has a great interactive map. The site is very pleasant to explore on foot. It's about 1½ km from the visitor entrance to the furthest ruins. A shuttle service in electric carts is available between the three main areas of the site (€5 per person): arrange pick-up times with the driver.

Santa Margherita di Belice
ⓘ *68 km east of Marsala.*

Fans of Giuseppe di Lampedusa's extraordinary novel *Il Gattopardo* (The Leopard) should make the pilgrimage to the quiet country town of Santa Margherita di Belice. The author spent idyllic childhood summers at his grandmother's palace, the Palazzo Filangeri-Cutò, which was the inspiration for Donnafugata in the novel. Sadly, the palace was destroyed by the 1968 earthquake, although remnants have been incorporated into the town hall, where a small museum contains the original manuscript, plus photographs and costumes. The ruins of the Baroque church of Santa Margherita, also described by Lampedusa, long left poignantly unroofed, are being converted into a **Museo della Memoria** ⓘ *Mon 0930-1400, 1530-1830, Tue, Wed and Fri 0900-1400, Sat-Sun 0930-1300, 1530 1830, free*, to those who lost their lives in the earthquake that shattered the valley on 15 January 1968.

Salemi and Gibellina

Sleepy little hilltop **Salemi** (45 km north of Mazara del Vallo) found itself briefly at the centre of the world's attention in 1860, when Garibaldi declared it the capital of newly unified Italy. Its moment of glory lasted just three days, but the event is commemorated in the Museo del Risorgimento, one of three small museums gathered together in the much-restored 13th-century **Castello di Salemi** ⓘ *T0924-982248, Tue-Sun 0900-1400, 1600-1900, free*. Salemi hit the news in 2008, when enterprising mayor Vittorio Sgarbi (an Italian TV personality) offered a thousand crumbling but historic houses for sale at just €1. The new **Museo della Mafia** ⓘ *via F D'Aguirres, Tue-Thu 1000-1300, 1600-1900, Fri-Sun 1000-1300, 1600-2000, €5*, in the former Collegio dei Gesuiti provides an often harrowing glimpse into the realities of the Mafia that is in gruesome contrast to the romanticised vision portrayed by Hollywood and the media. **Gibellina Nuovo**, 6 km east of Salemi, was supposed to be an ideal modern town, built by artists and architects after the terrible earthquake of 1968 devastated the original city. Unfortunately, the site is exposed and unshaded, and the construction proved to be so shoddy that the town, and all its famous public art, is literally falling apart. The ruins of old Gibellina, **Ruderi di Gibellina**, can be found 20 km east along the SS119 in the beautiful Val di Belice. The greenness is suddenly shattered by a sea of white cement smothering the hillside: this is Alberto Burri's controversial sculpture, *Cretto (Crevice)*, which covers the entire remains of the village.

Marsala and around listings

For hotel and restaurant price codes and other relevant information, see pages 11-16.

Where to stay

Marsala and around *p72*

€€€€ Kempinski Hotel Giardino di Costanza, *Via Salemi Km 7.1, Mazara del Vallo, T0923-675000, kempinski-sicily.com.* This was the fanciest resort on the island until the arrival of Rocco Forte's Verdara Resort, see page 86, but it's still gloriously relaxing and luxurious. There's a spa, a pool in tropical gardens, a children's programme, plus a choice of restaurants for fine dining, and even a private beach (a minibus makes the 15-minute drive).

€€ Carmine Hotel, *Piazza Carmine 16, T0923-711907, hotelcarmine.it.* A beautifully restored former convent, complete with original tiles and wooden beams, now houses this boutique hotel in Marsala. The nicest rooms have balconies overlooking the courtyard garden. Breakfast is served on a terrace gazing out over the gardens.

€ Hotel Centrale, *Via Salinisti 19, T0923-951777, hotelcentralemarsala.it.* A simple little two-star hotel in the heart of Marsala, this offers impeccably clean if functionally furnished rooms set around a plant-filled courtyard. It's a great deal with free bike hire and free parking.

€ Il Profumo del Sale, *Via Vaccari, 8, Marsala, T0923-189047, ilprofumodelsale.it.* A delightful little B&B in the heart of the old town, this has three simple but stylish rooms. Homemade bread and pastries are served for breakfast, and the lovely owner is full of helpful tips on where to eat and what to do.

€ La Finestra sul Sale, *Contrada Ettore Infersa 158, 5 km north of Marsala, near Isola San Pantaleo, T0923-733003, salineetoreinfersa.com.* This little B&B, just three rooms over a gloriously isolated café, is located by the pier where the boats leave for Mozia – there are spellbinding views over the lagoon. Midweek is best for quiet, but come at weekends (Thu-Sun) to enjoy live music at the nearby Caffè Mamma Caura, see page 78.

Self-catering

€ Baglio Calia, *Contrada Serroni, Mazara del Vallo, T0923-909390, bagliocalia.it.* A big, rambling country farm, this has been converted into a friendly *agriturismo*, with a range of apartments and bedrooms set in the converted outbuildings. It's 2 km from the centre of town, and from the beaches.

Restaurants

Marsala and around *p72*

€€€€ Il Pescatore, *Via Castelvetrano 191, Mazara del Vallo, T0923-947580, ristorantedelpescatore.com. Tue-Sun 1230-1500, 2000-2200.* Book early on summer weekends if you want one of the sought-after terrace tables at this restaurant on the outskirts of town, in a modern residential neighbourhood. Beautifully fresh fish is the highlight of the menu, including swordfish prepared in several different ways.

€€€ La Bettola, *Via Francesco Maccagnone 32, Mazara del Vallo, T0923-946422, ristorantelabettola.it. Thu-Tue 1300-1500, 1930-2200. Closed 2 weeks in Jul.* In the historic centre, with a small terrace behind wooden shades, this is an elegant spot for local cuisine. As you might expect in one of Italy's busiest fishing ports, the fish is superbly fresh; have it simply grilled, or in *ghiotto*, a sturdy fish stew.

€€€ Osteria Il Gallo e L'Innamorata, *Via S Bilardello 18, Marsala, T0923-195 4446, osteriailgalloelinnamorata.com. Wed-Mon 2000-2200.* A highly recommended choice in central Marsala, serving fish so fresh it melts in the mouth. Go for the bruschetta topped with *bottarga* (dried tuna roe, a pungent local speciality), and follow with pasta with *ragù di tonno* (when in season). Book in advance.

€€ Alla Kasbah, *Via Itria 10, Mazara del Vallo, T0923-906126. Tue-Sun 1300-1500, 1930-2230*. This popular trattoria is another excellent place to try western Sicily's signature dish, *cuscus di pesce*, prepared here with a slightly more exotic array of spices. Many of the recipes come from the island of Pantelleria and have a distinct North African influence.

€€ La Pineta, *Marinella di Selinunte, T0924-46820. Mid-Mar to end Sep 1000-2300 (hours erratic, advance booking advised)*. Dine with your toes in the sand at Bar Ristorante La Pineta, which is located east of Marinella di Selinunte in the Belice River nature reserve. Leave your car in the car park and follow the sandy path for the last 200 m. Try the spaghetti with *cozze* (mussels) and follow up with the fish of the day. May close in bad weather.

Cafés and bars

Enzo & Nino, *Via XI Maggio 130, Marsala, T0923-951969. Daily 0800-2000*. A long-established neighbourhood favourite on Marsala's main drag, this is an essential stop for coffee, snacks, or a refreshing ice cream.

Gelateria Coppetta, *Corso Umberto I 27, Mazara del Vallo, T0923-907337. Daily 1000-2200*. Among the flavours at this award-winning ice-cream parlour is luscious peach.

Caffè Mamma Caura, *Contrada Ettore Infersa, 5 km north of Marsala, near Isola San Pantaleo, T0923-966936. Summer daily 1000-0100, phone for winter opening hours*. Near the embarkation point for boats to Mozia, this charming and simple café-bar has magnificent views over the salt flats and is a romantic place to soak up the sunsets. Live jazz and pop at weekends.

Entertainment

Marsala and around *p72*
Cine Teatro Impero, *Piazza della Vittoria, Marsala. T0923-993393, comune.marsala.tp.it*. Cinema and theatre with all kinds of performances including regular concerts. Contact tourist office for info.

Festivals and events

Marsala and around *p72*
Estate a Marsala, *Marsala. Jul*. Outdoor concerts for the 'Summer in Marsala' festival (comune.marsala.tp.it).

Shopping

Marsala and around *p72*
E&N Pasticceria, *Via XI Maggio 130, Marsala, T0923-951969, pasticceriaen.com. Thu-Tue 0900-2000*. A selection of marzipan fruits, plus a mouthwatering range of traditional *dolci*. Try their *cassata*. Attached to popular café (see above).

Gerardi Gastronomia, *Piazza Mameli 14, Marsala, T0923-952240. Mon-Tue, Thu-Sat 0800-1300, 1630-2000, Wed 0800-1300*. A gourmet deli, with Sicilian and international fresh produce, including cheeses and hams.

What to do

Marsala and around *p72*
Cantine Florio, *Via Vincenzo Florio 1, T0923-781306, cantineflorio.it. Visits must be booked in advance, €5-10 depending on whether you choose the guided tour or not (tours must be booked in advance)*. The Marsala region has always been famous for its grapes but it was the Englishman John Woodhouse who saw the possibilities for a fortified-wine business and set up shop in 1773. By the end of the 18th century Marsala wine was being drunk on all of the British navy's ships. More British businesses, including Ingham, Good and Whitaker,

joined the industry, which peaked in the second half of the 19th century. The Florio family set up a firm in 1831, which was bought by Cinzano in 1924, along with the Woodhouse and Ingham-Whitaker wineries. The Cantine Florio, built of tufa stone in the 1830s, is now Marsala's biggest tourist attraction, with more than 30,000 visitors annually.

Feudo Bùcari, *Contrada Bùcari, Mazara del Vallo, T339-8662060, feudobucari.it*. Tastings and tours at this small but interesting winery, which produces some excellent reds, whites and the local Marsala.

Transport

Marsala and around *p72*
The centre of Marsala is small and compact. The bus station is on Piazza del Popolo, in the centre. The train station is on Viale Amerigo Fazio, about a 10-minute walk to the town centre. Regular bus and train services link it with Trapani and Mazara del Vallo. (Mazara, also easily negotiable on foot, is the starting point for buses to Selinunte, Ghibellina and Salemi.)

There are no direct trains from Palermo to Marsala; you will need to change at Trapani or Alcamo (average journey time is 3½ hrs). There are direct trains to Trapani and Mazara del Vallo. AST and Marinella buses link Mazara del Vallo with Marinella di Selinunte. There is only one bus a day from Marsala to Gibellina (1½ hrs) where there are connections for Salemi (20 mins from Gibellina). Gibellina is also served by buses from Alcamo (45 mins, 3 daily).

Directory

Marsala and around *p72*
Money Banco di Sicilia, via XI Maggio 91, T0923-766111. **Medical services Ospedale San Biagio**, piazza San Francesco 1, T0923-782111. **Farmacia Calcagno**, via XI Maggio 126, T0923-953254. **Post office** Via G Garibaldi 9, T0923-763014. **Tourist information** Via XI Maggio 100, T0923-714097, comune.marsala.tp.it.

Agrigento and around

Wrapped in the dirt-grey tentacles of a highway on stilts, Agrigento, at first glimpse, is a miserable sight. But hidden behind these concrete horrors is a rambling old town of cobbled streets and pretty squares high on a hilltop, and, strung out along a ridge dominating the valley below, the magnificent Valley of the Temples, a UNESCO World Heritage Site and the most impressive surviving temple complex outside mainland Greece. More superb archaeological sites dot this coast, including Eraclea Minoa, which boasts a panoramic theatre overlooking the sea. Further west, Sciacca is tucked behind medieval walls and overlooks a busy fishing port. Its long beaches of golden sand are a big favourite with Sicilian families.

Agrigento → *For listings, see pages 86-87.*

Ancient Akragas, which would become known as Agrigentum under the Romans, was one of the most powerful colonies of Magna Graecia. Brace yourself for the shocking intrusion of illegal construction, with shoddy concrete apartment buildings and hotels encroaching on the protected heritage site. This grim sight is relieved only by the orchards of almond trees, which burst into clouds of palest pink in February and March.

Valle dei Templi

ⓘ *Piazzale dei Templi, off the passeggiata Archeologica, T0922-497341, parcodeitempli.net, www.comune.agrigento.it. Collina dei Templi and Area di Zeus daily 0830-1 hr before dusk, €4.50/2 concession, or €6/4 for combined admission with archaeological museum; Giardino della Kolymbetra daily 1000-1 hr before dusk, €2. The Collina dei Templi (Temple Hill) is illuminated and open for evening visits Jul-mid-Sep Mon-Fri 1930-2130 and Sat-Sun 1930-2330, €10. See next page 'essentials', for more information.*

In the entire Mediterranean world, few sights evoke the splendour of ancient Greece like the great temple complex of Agrigento. Despite the name, the temples are actually set above the valley, where they loom imposingly from a high ridge and once beckoned to sailors. Sadly, creeping illegal development has substantially blighted their beauty, which once induced Goethe to sigh: "We shall never in our lives be able to rejoice again, after seeing such a stupendous view in this splendid valley." Akragas was founded in the sixth century BC, as a subcolony of Gela, but became one of the richest and most powerful colonies in Magna Graecia. After it was destroyed by the Carthaginians in 406 BC, it didn't regain its former influence until the Romans captured it in 210 BC and renamed it Agrigentum. At its height, Agrigento boasted a population of 200,000: four times the current number of inhabitants.

The finest surviving monuments of ancient Akragas are found along the via Sacra, where several temples in the Doric style were erected during the sixth and fifth centuries BC. Closest to the entrance gate by the piazzale dei Templi is the **Tempio di Ercole** (Temple of Heracles), whose eight intact columns were re-erected in the 1920s, while fragments of the rest are scattered nearby. Nearby, the pretty **Villa Aurea**, now a documentation and exhibition space, was the former home of Alexander Hardcastle (1872-1933), an Englishman who financed the reconstruction of the Tempio di Ercole and was made an honorary citizen of the city. Beyond it is the supremely graceful, golden **Tempio della Concordia** (Temple of Concord), which is the best preserved of the group, probably because it was converted into a Christian church in the sixth century AD. At the end of this section of the via Sacra is the **Tempio di Giunone** (Temple of Hera/Juno), smaller than the Temple of Concord but remarkably intact and exquisitely located. This trio is spectacular in the evening, burnished gold by the setting sun and beautifully illuminated after nightfall. There are two more temples at the other end of the via Sacra, accessed via a gate on the piazzale dei Templi. The massive stones on the right are all that remain of the **Tempio di Giove Olimpico** (Temple of Olympian Zeus/Jupiter), which archaeologists believe was once the largest Doric temple ever built (although it was never completed). Beyond it are the remnants of the **Tempio di Castore e Polluce** (Temple of Castor and Pollux), with a group of columns re-erected in the early 19th century.

An entrance near the Temple of Olympian Zeus/Jupiter leads to the **Giardino della Kolymbetra** (Kolymbetra Garden), the most recent archaeological area to be opened to visitors, and perhaps the most poetic. It was once a beautiful lake, dug out by slaves for the tyrant Theron, and surrounded by gardens, but it was later filled in and then used as an orchard by the Arabs. Now, huge stones are half-hidden by luxuriant greenery, and trees frame beautiful views of the distant temples.

Valle dei Templi essentials The main area of the archaeological park is divided into three sections: the Collina dei Templi, the Area di Zeus and the Giardino dell Kolymbetra. The first two are accessed with the same ticket, while the Kolymbetra Garden has separate admission. The main entrance gates to all three sections are on the piazzale dei Templi, passeggiata Archeologica, 2 km from the centre: take city buses 1, 2 or 3 from outside the train station. There is also a small ticket office at the eastern end of the via Sacra, near the Temple of Hera, on the via Panoramica dei Templi. There is a small café at the main entrance, and another on the via Sacra by the Temple of Hera. More ruins, including the Hellenistic-Roman district, are located near the archaeological museum. This is not open to the public but can be viewed from the road.

Museo Regionale Archeologico
ⓘ *Contrada San Nicola, via dei Templi, T0922-401565, parcovalledeitempli.it. Tue-Sat 0900-1900, Sun-Mon 0900-1300, €4.50/2 concession or €6/4 for combined admission ticket with Valle dei Templi, €5 audio guide.*

Agrigento's excellent archaeological museum is bright, modern and – almost uniquely in Sicily – provides visitor information in several languages. The museum is organized chronologically and contains finds dating back to the earliest Neolithic settlements, as well as those from ancient Akragas and other important Greek colonies in the region, such as Gela and Eraclea Minoa. In **Room III**, there is an outstanding collection of red-figure and black-figure Attic vases from the sixth to fifth centuries BC, including the famous *Crater of Dionysios*. **Room VI** contains the huge *telamones* (colossal human figures) which once decorated the massive temple of Olympian Zeus. One, which is more than 7 m high, has been reconstructed from the remnants found at the site, while three massive heads sit by the wall. **Room X** contains the famous marble statue of *Ephebus of Agrigento*, a young athlete who lived in the fifth century BC. There are Roman sarcophagi in **Room XI**, including a tiny one which belonged to a child, and a red-figured crater from Gela in **Room XV**.

The museum sits in a garden next to the graceful 13th-century **church of San Nicola**. This was built with volcanic rock taken from the great Temple of Olympian Zeus, and contains a beautiful Roman sarcophagus of white marble, depicting the tragic story of Phaedra and Hippolytus. Excavations next to the museum have revealed the remnants of the **Bouleuterion**, which housed the *boule*, or council of citizens. Across the main road, the fenced-off remains of the Hellenistic-Roman quarter can be viewed from a distance. This residential area was probably developed from the second century BC (first by the Greeks and then by the Romans) and it's possible to make out the remnants of houses with mosaic decoration and even heating arrangements.

Agrigento town
The Greek acropolis once occupied the hilltop where Agrigento's old town is now clustered. Barbarian invasions and pirate raids sent the local inhabitants scuttling up from the valley below, and a walled city developed first under the Saracens and then the Normans. Although Agrigento's old town now draws visitors on their way to the temples, rather

than for any intrinsic attractions, it is still an enjoyable spot for an amble. From the central piazza Vittorio Emanuele, the via Atenea begins its sinuous ascent. This is the heart of local life, a (usually) pedestrianized street lined with shops, cafés and *pasticcerie*. Off the via Atenea is the **Monastero di Santo Spirito** ⓘ *Salida Santo Spirito, T0922-590371*, a medieval complex containing a florid Baroque church (usually closed) and a **folk museum** ⓘ *Mon-Fri 0900-1300, €2.50*; just off the cloister, you can order delicious almond and pistachio *dolci* baked by the nuns. The grand 19th-century **Teatro Pirandello** is named after Agrigento's most famous son, Luigi Pirandello, whose birthplace is the **Casa Natale di Luigi Pirandello** ⓘ *4 km from Agrigento, Contrada Caos Villaseta, T0922-511826, daily 0900-1330 and 1430-1900, €4/2*. The 13th-century **Chiesa di Santa Maria dei Greci** was built over the ruins of an ancient Greek temple; the recycled columns are visible in the nave. At the very top of town, up an impressive flight of steps, the severe lines of Agrigento's **Cattedrale di San Gerlando** ⓘ *via Duomo, T0922-490011, usually open for mass only*, betray its 12th-century Norman origins, although it was significantly remodelled in the 16th and 17th centuries.

Around Agrigento → *For listings, see pages 86-87.*

East to Gela
Ferries for the Pelagie Islands depart from busy **Porto Empedocle**, which was named after the Greek philosopher Empedocles but has recently become famous for its association with another writer, Andrea Camilleri, who was born here in 1925. The town, in its fictional guise of Vigàta, serves as the setting for novels featuring Camilleri's most popular creation, the detective and gourmand Salvo Montelbano. Just west of Porto Empedocle, there is a popular beach by the stunning **Scala dei Turchi**, a huge 'staircase' of the palest stone which has been eroded by the wind and time. Heading east towards Gela, there are more wild and beautiful coves to be found at the base of the Punta Bianca, and near the little resort of **Marina di Palma**. The coastal SS115 continues to **Licata**, a large, shabby seaport, with a sprinkling of archaeological remains from ancient **Phintias**, and a likeable, if unremarkable, old centre. Gourmets take note: this humble town is home to what many consider to be the best restaurant on Sicily (see page 86). There are some attractive dune-backed beaches on the quiet coastline between Licata and Gela, including one overlooked by a castle at **Falconara** and another, with a couple of beach bars, at **Manfria**.

North of Agrigento
Some 14 km northeast of Agrigento, **Favara** is a handsome little town, with a clutch of Baroque monuments overlooking the central piazza Cavour. Nearby, lost in the hills, **Naro** dominates the surrounding countryside from its lofty hilltop. Now a quiet agricultural town overlooking a huge reservoir, it was once a medieval citadel prized for its strategic location. A sturdy 14th-century castle and a handful of faded *palazzi* and churches are poignant reminders of its glorious past. Perhaps the strangest sight around Agrigento is the black, bubbling landscape of the **Vulcanelli di Maccalube** (15 km north of Agrigento, 3 km outside Aragona). These strange craters belch black clay every few seconds, creating mini-volcanoes up to a metre high and intricate patterns in the sun-baked soil.

West to Sciacca
Back along the coast, **Siculiana** (18 km west of Agrigento) sits on a gentle hill overlooking the sea, surrounded by lush fields of grapes, olives and wheat. The town is topped by the

Five of the best beaches

Marina di Palma The stretch of coast near Marina di Palma is characterized by cliffs pierced with a series of delightful, pebbly coves overlooking transparent waters.

Oasi WWF di Torre Salsa Wild, sandy beaches backed by dunes, part of a nature reserve.

Eraclea Minoa Quite possibly the most photographed beach in southern Sicily, this is backed by pine forest and tall, white cliffs.

Sciacca Sciacca's town beach has great facilities, shallow waters, and swathes of pale sand, making it perfect for families.

Spiaggia dei Conigli, Lampedusa The most famous beach on the island, where the loggerhead turtles come to breed, and where tourists roast on the whitest, finest sand in Sicily.

---

huge Baroque Chiesa Madre. The sandy beaches between Siciliana Marina and Realmonte are beautiful, and a section, the **Oasi WWF di Torre Salsa** ⓘ *T0922-818220, wwftorresalsa.it*, is protected as a nature reserve by the WWF. Loggerhead turtles nest on the beaches, which are virtually empty for most of the year.

Eraclea Minoa
ⓘ *Contrada Minoa, Eraclea Minoa, T0922-846005. Daily 0900-1900 in summer, otherwise until 1 hr before dusk, €4/2 concession. It is signposted off the SS115/E931, 6 km west of Siciliana Marina.*

The isolated ruins of ancient Eraclea Minoa are magnificently set on a lonely clifftop overlooking the brilliant blue sea. According to legend, King Minos of Crete landed here in pursuit of Daedalus, who had helped Theseus and Ariadne find their way out of the labyrinth. The local king refused to hand over Daedalus, and murdered Minos instead. This panoramic spot was inhabited in Neolithic times, and it was a Phoenician settlement before Greeks from Selinunute arrived in the sixth century BC. It was conquered by the Romans during the third century BC, but gradually declined over the following centuries. The theatre, built in the third century BC, is the best surviving monument, poised on the cliff edge, and still occasionally used for performances. A museum on site contains finds from the excavations. Below the ruins, there is a stunning, long sandy beach backed by pines, and more secluded coves around the headland of Capo Bianco.

Sciacca
ⓘ *61 km northwest of Agrigento.*

Sciacca was founded by the Greeks in the fifth century BC as a spa town for nearby Selinunte; its pungent, sulphurous waters are still believed to possess curative properties. The lovely old town, a tumble of narrow streets overlooking a colourful fishing port, is tucked behind the remnants of 15th-century walls. At the centre of town, the expansive piazza Scandaliato – dotted with palm trees and with pretty views of the higgledy-piggledy harbour and out to sea – is the focal point of the evening *passeggiata*. On the outskirts of town, Sciaccamare is a popular holiday resort, with ranks of concrete hotels overlooking sandy beaches.

Just east of town, signposted off the SS15, the **Castello Incantato** ⓘ *'Enchanted Castle', Tue-Sat 0900-1300, 1500-1700 (summer 1600-2000), €3*, is actually an old *baglio* (country house), once inhabited by Filippo Bentivegna, who went to America to seek his fortune, and fell in love but was badly beaten by a rival. He returned to Sciacca *'non proprio sano di mente'* (not quite right in the head), as the tourist office frankly puts it, and began to create a fantastical and alluring sculpture garden, chiselling strange stone busts of everyone from his former love to Mussolini and Garibaldi.

Agrigento and around listings

For hotel and restaurant price codes and other relevant information, see pages 11-16.

Where to stay

Agrigento and around *p80*

€€€€ Rocco Forte Verdura Golf and Spa Resort, *SS 115 Km 131, Sciacca, T0925-998001, verdararesort.com*. The island's most luxurious resort opened in 2010 and offers all the amenities you'd expect: a private beach, two of Italy's top golf courses, several restaurants, a spectacular spa, special family programmes, facilities for watersports and much more.

€€€-€€ Falconara Charming Resort, *Località Falconara, Butera, T0934-349012. Open May-Sep*. On the seafront, about 8 km east of Licata, this 'chic' hotel occupies a modern complex adjoining the (private) Norman castle that guards the headland. It's a small resort, offering tennis, a pool, small spa and a private beach, but your own transport is recommended if you want to explore the area.

€ Hotel Amici, *Acrone 5, Agrigento, T0922-402831, hotelamici.com*. Simple rooms with air conditioning plus a convenient location near the train station make this budget hotel a good bet. The buses for the Valley of the Temples depart from close by. Triple and quadruple rooms also available.

€ Camere a Sud B&B, *Via Ficani 6, off via Alenea, Agrigento, T349-638 4424, camereasud.it*. Tucked away in the heart of Agrigento's old quarter, this arty little B&B has just three pretty rooms (two doubles and a triple), all with air conditioning and en suite bathrooms. Breakfast is served on a tiny terrace overlooking the rooftops.

€ Camera con Vista, *Via Porta Aurea 4, Agrigento, T0922-554605, cameraconvista.it*. Many hotels promise views of Agrigento's famous temples, but few actually deliver: this inn has views over the valley to the temples high on their imposing ridge. The eight rooms are simply furnished but all have fridges and air conditioning, and most boast balconies or terraces on which you can soak up the views.

€ Terrazze di Montelusa B&B, *Piazza Lena 6, Agrigento, T0922-28556, terrazzedimontelusa.it*. This elegant B&B in a 19th-century town house in Agrigento's old quarter contains three bedrooms, two suites (for only €10 extra) and welcoming owners. A delicious breakfast is served on a panoramic terrace, with views stretching down to the temples and out to sea.

Self-catering

€€ Mandranova, *Palma di Montechiaro, SS115 Km 217, T393-986 2169, mandranova.it*. This *agriturismo* with restaurant is located amid olive groves, a 20-minute drive from Agrigento (the main coast road is by the gate – a blessing and a curse). Choose from a traditionally furnished room in the main house or the converted former railway station, or self-catering accommodation in a separate villa (sleeps up to six, weekly rates €1000-2700). There are gardens, a small pool, a restaurant, and cookery lessons.

Fattoria Mosè, *Via M Pascal 4, Agrigento, T0922-606115, fattoriamose.com*. Peacefully located about 4 km from the Valley of the Temples and 3 km from the sea, this *agriturismo* offers rooms (half-board only) in the owners' 19th-century manor house or self-catering in apartments (sleeping two to six people, €500-1100 per week, one week minimum in high season). The farm produces organic citrus fruits and olive oil and a home-cooked dinner can be prepared.

Restaurants

Agrigento and around *p80*

€€€€ La Madia, *22 Corso Filippo di Re Capriata, Licata, T0922-771443, ristorantelamadia.it*. Mon, Wed-Sun

1300-1530, 1930-2200; also closed Sun lunch in Aug. This restaurant has won countless awards, including two Michelin stars for chef Pino Cuttaia, and the Best Restaurant in Sicily award for several consecutive years. Go for the smoked cod with pine nuts, or the couscous with plump Sicilian prawns. Around €80-90 per head, booking recommended.

€€€ Hosteria del Vicolo, *Vicolo Sammaritano 10, Sciacca, T0925-23071. Tue-Sun 1230-1530, 1930-2200*. A local classic in the historic heart of Sciacca. Its refined cuisine takes traditional Sicilian recipes and reinvents them with contemporary flair.

€€ Spizzulio, *Via Panoramica dei Templi 23, Agrigento, T0922-20712, spizzulio.it. Mon-Sat 1900-2300*. An intimate *enoteca*, serving Sicilian wines, platters of charcuterie, cheeses and olives, as well as a selection of more substantial dishes.

Cafés and bars

Infurna Pasticceria, *Via Atenea 96, Agrigento, T0922-595959. Mon-Sat 0900-2100, Sun 1230-1900*. A good place for cappuccino and some pistachio cream-filled *cornetti* before hitting the sights.

Festivals and events

Agrigento and around *p80*
Rappresentazioni Pirandelliane, *Jun-Aug*. Agrigento's summer-long drama festival dedicated to the works of Luigi Pirandello.

Shopping

Agrigento and around *p80*
Ceramics
Ceramiche Cascio, *Corso V Emanuele 115, Sciacca, T0925-82829. Mon-Sat 0900-1300, 1700-1900*. Sciacca is famous for its ceramics, and this is just one of many craft shops.

Food and drink
Salumeria del Buon Sapore, *Via Cappuccini 20, Agrigento, T0925-26562.* *Mon-Sat 0900-1300, 1630-1900*. Cured hams and sausages, cheeses, oils, wines and much more.

Transport

Agrigento and around *p80*
There are daily train services between Agrigento and Palermo (2 hrs 10 mins), and Caltanissetta (1 hr 30 mins). The main train station (**Agrigento Centrale**) is conveniently central on piazza Guglielmo Marconi.

The main inter-urban bus station is on Piazzale Rosselli. Different companies run services to most Sicilian cities, including Palermo (**Cuffaro**, T0922-418231, cuffaro.com, 2 hrs) and Catania (**SAIS**, T0922-595260, saisautolinee.it, 3 hrs), and to Palermo airport (**Sal**, T0922-401360, autolineesal.it). Sal also run services between Agrigento, Porto Empedocle, Licata and Gela.

Local buses depart from the piazza Marconi, outside the train station. While the historic centre of Agrigento is small and easy to walk around (if rather steep in places), the Valley of the Temples is 2 km from the centre – it's served by city buses 1, 2 or 3, which leave regularly from piazza Marconi.

Directory

Agrigento and around *p80*
Money ATMs at **Banco di Sicilia**, Piazza S Francesco d;Assisi, T0922-24113; **Banco d'Italia**, via Crispi Francesco 6, T0922-20909. **Medical services** Ospedale S Giovanni di Dio, Contrada Consolida, T0922-442111, aspag.it. **Farmacia Averna Dottor Antonio**, via Atenea 325, T0922-26093 (Mon-Sat 0900-1300, 1700-1930). **Post office** Piazza Vittorio Emanuele 7, T0922-551111 (Mon-Fri 0800-1330, Sat 0800-1230). **Tourist information** AAPIT, viale della Vittoria 225, T0922-401352; AAST, via Cesare Battisti 15, T0922-20454.

Contents

90 History
- 90 Early Sicily
- 91 Greek Sicily
- 92 Roman and Byzantine Sicily
- 93 Medieval Sicily: from Arab to Spanish rule
- 94 Bourbon Sicily and Italian Unification
- 96 Modern Sicily

Background

History

Early Sicily

The earliest settlements in Sicily date back to around 10,000-8000 BC. The oldest surviving evidence of these early peoples are the delicate cave paintings found at the Grotto dell'Addaura on the outskirts of Palermo and in the Grotta del Genovese on the island of Lévanzo. The paintings depict deer, among other animals, which were the main source of food and skins. By around 6000 BC, settled agriculture was introduced to Sicily, probably by farmers from the eastern Mediterranean, who began to produce wheat and grain, and to raise sheep and goats.

Imported tools and pottery designs indicate that trade with other Mediterranean peoples was becoming increasingly common by 2500 BC. From around 1500 BC, there is evidence of substantial contact with the Minoan culture (modern Crete). The Mycenaens, from their home in the Greek Peloponnese, established a flourishing trade in obsidian (a hard, black volcanic glass) with the Aeolian Islands between 1600 and 1150 BC. Ancient artefacts from this period can be found in the excellent Museo Archeologico Regionale Eoliano in Lipari. Other settlements, notably Thapsos near modern Siracusa, prospered thanks to trans-Mediterranean trade.

Sicani, Sicels and Elymians

Among the earliest indigenous peoples in Sicily were the Sicani, who originally occupied the northwestern part of the island. They shifted eastwards with the arrival of the Elymians in around 1100 BC, although there is no evidence of conflict between the two tribes. It's uncertain where the Elymians came from, although historians believe that Anatolia in modern Turkey or the Aegean seem most likely. Thucydides, the Greek historian (460-395 BC), would later claim that their ancestors were refugees from Troy. The Elymians established settlements in western Sicily, notably at Erice and Segesta while eastern Sicily was largely occupied by the Sicels. The Sicels arrived around 1200 BC from what is now mainland Italy, and would eventually give their name to the island, *Sicilia*. The Sicels brought iron to Bronze Age Sicily and introduced the domesticated horse. They were also responsible for the vast necropolis at Pantalica, a UNESCO World Heritage Site, with more than 5,000 tombs gouged into a cliff face.

Phoenicians

Trading collapsed in the Mediterranean after the demise of the Mycenean civilization some time around 1100 BC and Sicily remained isolated for about three centuries. However, from the 11th century BC the Phoenicians began to explore the western Mediterreanean from their homelands on the Levantine coast (on the land now occupied by parts of modern Lebanon, Syria and Israel). Their first trading partners were the Greeks, to whom they sold a rare purple dye made from crushed shells; it was the Greeks who gave the Levantine traders the name Phoenicians, which means 'purple people'. From the eighth century BC, the Phoenicians began to establish trading posts along the Sicilian coast, most notably at Motya (modern Mozia), Solus (modern Soluto) and Panormos (modern Palermo). They also introduced the Phoenician alphabet, which is considered the basis for Greek and Roman letters. The Phoenicians enjoyed peaceful relations with the Elymians and other local tribes, but trouble was on the horizon. Where the Phoenician traders led, the Greeks would follow, and the first Greek colonizers arrived on eastern Sicily in the eighth century BC.

In the sixth century BC, the Phoenician homeland on the Levantine coast was conquered by the Persians and absorbed into the Persian empire. Many Phoenicians fled across the ocean to Carthage (modern Tunis), which would become the centre of a mighty maritime empire – and a deadly rival to Greece. The Phoenican settlements on western Sicily fell to the Carthaginians, who developed them into walled cities. It was only a matter of time before the Greeks and Carthaginians would clash over territorial and trading rights.

Greek Sicily

The first permanent Greek colony in Sicily was established in Naxos in 735 BC. During the following century or so, several more would follow: first were those among the eastern coast including Siraco (Syracuse) in 734 or 733 BC, Zancle or Messene (Messina) in 730 BC, and Katane (Catania) in 729 BC. When the best sites on the eastern coast were taken, the settlers moved to the southern coast of the island and established themselves at Selinus (Selinunte) in 630 BC, Gela in 688 BC, and Akragas (Agrigento, see page 81) in 580 BC. The Greeks also absorbed several Sicel cities, including Enna, which became identified with the Persephone myth.

Akragas rapidly became one of the largest and richest of the new city states, and erected the magnificent temple complex at the Valle dei Templi (see page 81). As the early settlements developed, the Greeks grew bolder, and Dorius of Sparta attempted to establish a colony on Carthaginian territory in western Sicily 514 BC. He was quickly ousted, but the Greeks and Carthaginians began to prepare for combat. The Carthaginians were crushed by Gelon, the powerful tyrant (leader) of Gela and Syracuse, in the battle of Himera in 480 BC, but the Greeks faced new problems with a Sicel uprising led by Ducetius in 452 BC. When the Peloponnesian War (431-404 BC) broke out between Athens and Sparta, Syracuse, allied with Sparta, was on the front line. The Athenians sent a vast fleet, the doomed Sicilian Expedition, to take the island in 415 BC, but were spectacularly defeated. The Carthaginians returned to take their revenge for Himera, which they destroyed in 409 BC, before sacking Akragas (Agrigento) in 406 BC.

Another tyrant emerged in Syracuse: Dionysos I (432-367 BC) took advantage of the confusion to sieze power in 405 BC. He would make Syracuse the greatest city of Magna Graecia, but was known for his cruelty. Tyrant meant simply 'leader' at this time, but Dionysos I was worthy of its modern definitions of despot and oppressor. Dionysos conquered territories across Sicily and southern Italy, and kept the Carthaginians at bay – not least by the erection of mighty walls and the great fortress at the Castello Eurialo – but was eventually poisoned by his own son (according to one account of his death). Dionysos II (c397-343 BC) was a weak ruler and Syracuse collapsed into anarchy. The Corinthians sent Timoleon (c411-337 BC) to impose order, and democratic law was restored in 339 BC.

Meanwhile, the Carthaginians were once again causing trouble. They were defeated in 341 BC, but the death of Timoleon plunged the region back into chaos. A general from Himera, Agothocles, assumed power but achieved little and was assasinated in 289 BC. Several Greek city states including Taormina asked Pyrrhus of Epirus to drive out the Carthaginians in 278 BC. In 277 BC, he captured the Carthaginian stronghold of Eryx (modern Erice), but was forced to leave the island after the Carthaginians refused to relinquish their other settlements, and the locals turned against him.

In Messina, an apparently minor crisis would have dramatic repercussions. The Mamertines, former mercenaries who had been granted the city by Agothocles, asked both Carthage and the emerging powers in Rome for support in their struggle with Syracuse. The Carthaginians established a garrison in Messina, but relations between Carthage and Rome, former allies, had deteriorated and the Romans sent an expedition force to Sicily in 264 BC. Thus began the First Punic War (264-241 BC), the first of three major wars fought between Carthage (*Punicus* in Latin, referring to the Phoenician ancestry of the Carthaginians) and the Roman Republic. Hieron II of Syracuse, tyrant from 270-215 BC, negotiated a treaty with the Romans, and, under his rule, Syracuse enjoyed a long period of peace and prosperity. Hieron II was succeeded by Hieronymous, aged just 15, who broke the alliance with Rome and asked the Carthaginians, who had gained some notable victories in the Second Punic War (218-201 BC), for support. In response, the Romans set siege to Syracuse, which held out for almost three years before finally falling in 212 BC.

Roman and Byzantine Sicily

Sicily became the first Roman overseas province, and was ruled from Syracuse, the capital of the island, by a Roman *praetor* (governor). The city states remained more or less intact, but were required to pay heavy taxes, which took the form of grain, to the empire.

The population of Rome was growing rapidly (even conservative estimates place it at around 1 million), and grain was needed urgently. Sicily would become Rome's 'bread basket'. To this end, the land was expropriated and then parcelled out to new owners favoured by Rome. The Romans became the first of a long line of foreign invaders to ruthlessly exploit Sicily. The local people, who had farmed the land for five centuries, were now dependent on rich, and usually foreign, landowners. The Romans stripped the island of trees, using the timber to build ships, and making more land available for cultivation.

As the number of landholdings increased, more slaves were imported to work in the fields. Thousands of slaves arrived after Carthage (modern Tunis) was razed in 145 BC, at the end of the Third (and final) Punic War (149-146 BC). The wealthy landowners of Sicily were growing richer at the expense of a large and increasingly embittered slave class, who were treated with exceptional brutality. The first Slave Revolt (136-132 BC) was led by Eunus of Enna, whose followers managed to occupy a large swathe of central Sicily before being savagely put down by the Roman army. Another revolt, which took place near Palermo (104-100 BC), was smaller but concluded no less tragically: the slaves were promised mercy if they capitulated, but were sent, instead, to Rome to be torn apart by lions.

Politically, Sicily was a quiet backwater under Roman rule, but it found itself centre stage briefly during the civil wars of the first century BC. Julius Caesar (100-44 BC) had nominated Octavian (63 BC to AD 14) – later known as Augustus – as his successor, but Octavian's claim was challenged by Pompey, who was supported by the Sicilians. After Pompey's defeat, the Sicilians were punished: the entire population of Tauromenium (Taormina) was expelled, numerous other city states lost their privileges, and large swathes of land were expropriated as imperial estates.

From the first century AD, much larger landholdings developed, called *latifundia*, which relied heavily on vast amounts of slave labour. Local smallholders were forced to find other occupations, as their land was swallowed up by the great estates, and the inland towns declined notably as the rural population migrated to the coastal cities. However, the wealthy landowners lived in considerable splendour, as evidenced by the dazzling mosaic decoration of the Villa Romana del Casale in Piazza Armerina.

Rise of Christianity

Sicily was one of the first Roman regions to become Christianized. St Paul preached in Syracuse in around AD 52, and two of the earliest Christian martyrs were Sant'Agata of Catania (AD 230-251) and Santa Lucia of Syracuse (AD 283-304). Although Christians were persecuted for many years, by AD 380 the official religion of the Roman Empire was Christianity.

By the late third century AD, Diocletian had divided the vast and unwieldy Roman Empire into east and west, each administered by an emperor. The practice continued erratically for a century, but Theodosius (AD 347-395) was the last emperor to rule both eastern and western portions. After his death, the Empire would split decisively, with the Eastern Roman Empire ruling independently from its capital at Constantinople (modern Istanbul), which had been founded in AD 324.

Several Germanic tribes flooded into the declining Western Empire's territories on the Italian peninsula. In AD 440, the Vandals landed on Sicily, only to be ousted in AD 476 by the Ostrogoths. The Goths remained until AD 535, when the island was recovered by the Byzantines (by which name the former Eastern Roman Empire would become known) in AD 535. From AD 663 to AD 668, Syracuse had another moment of glory, when it briefly became the capital of the Empire under Constans II. It was also appointed metropolis of the whole Sicilian Church. In AD 652, an Arab force landed briefly, but soon left. They would return again to conquer the island in the ninth century.

Medieval Sicily: from Arab to Spanish rule

Arab invasion

A Byzantine governor, Euphemius, proclaimed himself emperor in Syracuse in around AD 826. He was rapidly ousted, and fled to north Africa, where he asked the Arabs for support. In AD 827, Euphemius returned to Sicily with a vast fleet and more than 10,000 men under the command of Asad ibn al-Furat, but his own ambitions ended when he was killed later that year. The Arabs, who had conquered huge Mediterranean territories including most of the Iberian peninsula in the preceding century, had long dreamed of ruling Sicily. Palermo (called Bal'harm under the Arabs) fell in AD 831; Messina in AD 842; Enna in AD 859; Syracuse in AD 878; Catania in AD 900; and the last Byzantine stronghold at Taormina, in AD 902.

Sicily had suffered famine and depopulation before the arrival of the Arabs, who revitalized the island's economy by introducing mulberries for silk-making, as well as oranges, pistachios and sugar cane. The Sicilian Emirate allowed freedom of worship to the native Christians, but levied a special tax for the privilege. By AD 902, Palermo had replaced Syracuse as Sicily's capital, and was considered one of the most beautiful and cultured cities of the Mediterranean. But, only a century later, the Emirate was destabilized by dynastic disputes, and the Arab leaders of Catania and Agrigento hired Norman mercenaries to support them in battle. The battle was won, but the Normans, who had already conquered much of southern Italy, didn't leave.

Norman Sicily (1091-1194)

Led by the brothers Robert Guiscard and Roger Hauteville, later Roger I of Sicily, the Normans took Messina in 1061, Syracuse in 1086, and Palermo in 1072. Roger was invested as Count of Sicily, and the entire island was under Norman control by 1091. Roger's son, Roger II of Sicily (1095-1154), would unite all the Norman conquests in Italy into one kingdom with a strong, centralized government. Under his enlightened rule, the Kingdom of Sicily enjoyed a golden age, particularly in the arts, and its extraordinary mix of peoples – Byzantine Greeks, Muslim Arabs, Jews, Normans, Lombards and Sicilians – coexisted peacefully. However, under Norman rule, Roman Catholicism would become the predominant religion, partly owing to considerable Lombard immigration from northern Italy. When Roger II's grandson, William II (Guglielmo II, 1155-1189), known as 'The Good', died without issue, the throne of Sicily was claimed by Henry VI (1165-1197), of the German Hohenstaufen dynasty, rulers of the Holy Roman Empire. He was succeeded by his son Frederick II (1194-1250), who became King of Sicily at the age of four.

Hohenstaufen and Angevin rule (1194-1282)

Frederick II (Federico II) was known as '*Stupor mundi*' ('Wonder of the world'), and his court at Palermo was famous for its magnificence and academia. He was locked in continuous battles with the papacy throughout much of his reign (paid for partly by heavy taxation on the Sicilians), and constructed a chain of mighty fortresses across the island. The premature death of Frederick's son precipitated another succession crisis, which ended when Sicily came briefly under Angevin rule (1266-1282). Charles of Anjou was deeply unpopular with Sicilians, and the crushing taxation imposed by his French officials further alienated locals. They revolted in 1282, in the uprising known as the Sicilian Vespers (triggered outside a church in Palermo, when a French soldier dared to address a Sicilian woman), during which thousands of French inhabitants were massacred. The Sicilians begged Peter III of Aragon (1239-1285) – Peter the Great – for help. After ousting the Angevins, he was crowned King of Sicily, initiating over 400 years of Spanish rule.

Spanish rule (1282-1713)

For much of the 14th century, Sicily was ruled as an independent kingdom, and a sense of a Sicilian nationhood began to emerge. Catalan (spoken by the Aragonese) was the language of the court, but Sicilian was spoken in parliament and by the people. When Aragon became part of Spain (through marriage) in 1409, the Sicilian crown passed with it. Once again, Sicily was reduced to an unimportant backwater, governed by a viceroy and a handful of feudal barons. The Black Death reached Europe through Messina in 1347, and famine, revolt and epidemics continued throughout the 15th century. In 1492, Muslims and Jews were expelled from all Spanish dominions, including Sicily. Another outbreak of plague in 1656 decimated the island's population (Trapani was completely abandoned), and a terrible earthquake shattered the eastern portion of the island in 1693, killing more than 60,000 people. Several cities, notably Catania and Noto, were handsomely rebuilt in the Sicilian Baroque style. In 1713, the Spanish lost Sicily at the conclusion of the War of the Spanish Succession (1701-1714), and the island passed briefly to Savoy (1713-1720), then to the Austrian Habsburgs (1720-1735), and finally to the Bourbons of Naples in 1735.

Bourbon Sicily and Italian Unification

Bourbon rule (1735-1860)

The Bourbon King Charles V (who would become Carlos III of Spain in 1759) made some efforts at dismantling Sicily's anachronistic feudalism and modernizing its agriculture, but had little success. The status quo remained unchanged: the barons owned the land, which was farmed by the poor, who were entirely dependent on their overlords. The old-fashioned farming methods resulted in poor yields, and most Sicilians lived at subsistence level. When the harvest failed, famine ensued: 30,000 people died in 1763 alone. Charles V and his son Ferdinand (who would become known as Ferdinand I of the Two Sicilies) attempted to alleviate the problem by banishing the Jesuits in 1759, and offering their land for sale in smaller parcels. Unfortunately, the poor still couldn't afford it, so the land was snapped up by the barons. Several reforms were enacted under Viceroy Caracciolo, who crushed the Inquisition (which had become yet another weapon in the armoury of the manipulative barons), but he was forced to resign after the Palermitani revolted when he tried to shorten the religious festival in honour of Santa Rosalia, their patron saint.

The court remained at Naples, capital of the Kingdom of the Two Sicilies (comprising the island and southern Italy). Although largely indifferent to the fate of the island, the royal family were forced to move briefly to Palermo in 1799, and again between 1806 and 1815, when their capital was threatened during the Napoleonic Wars. As Ferdinand II was unable to raise an army in Sicily, they were protected by the British military, notably Lord Nelson, who was handsomely rewarded with a large estate in Bronte, near Mount Etna. The Sicilians were impressed by the British (not least for the cash they brought to the island), and some nobles even raised the possibility of annexing the island to Britain. They also asked for British help drafting the new Constitution in 1812; Ferdinand, threatened with a French invasion and pressured by the irksome presence of the British protectors, was forced to accept it. Under the Constitution, Sicily was granted independence, and the parliament was allowed to make laws and raise taxes. Most importantly, the feudal system was abolished, and landowners were finally required to pay taxes.

Once the Napoleonic threat diminished and Ferdinand was back in Naples, the Constitution was quickly repealed, but the issue of Sicilian independence gained increasing acceptance. Angered by Bourbon neglect, the Sicilians revolted several times, most significantly in 1820 and in 1848, Europe's 'year of revolutions'. Ferdinand was once again forced to accept the 1812 Constitution but, after just 16 months of heady independence, he sent in the army. Messina and Palermo were subjected to such heavy bombardment that Ferdinand was nicknamed 'King Bomba', but he had control of the island once again.

Union with Italy

Dissatisfaction with Bourbon rule was increasingly underpinned by a growing nationalism, and the Italian peninsula was caught up in the wars and struggles of the Risorgimento ('the revival'), a radical movement dedicated to the reunification of Italy. In 1860, Giuseppe Garibaldi (1807-1882), who had enjoyed considerable success against the Austrians and the French in the north of Italy, led his troops against the Bourbons. He took Palermo and Messina, gaining the support of the Sicilian peasants by promising land reform. But land reform had to wait, while Garibaldi crossed to the mainland to take Naples and defeat the Bourbons, and the peasants grew impatient. Rebellion broke out as the peasants attempted to take land by force, particularly at Bronte, but were rapidly put down. In 1861 Italian Unification was officially complete, and the Piedmontese Victor Emmanuel II was proclaimed King of all Italy.

Garibaldi believed Sicily deserved regional autonomy within the new Italian nation, but it quickly became apparent that the politicians in Turin thought differently. Sicily, like the rest of Italy, was taxed heavily and conscription was imposed. Garibaldi confiscated church land in order to give it to the poor, but Turin was desperate for money and sold it to the highest bidder. The Sicilians found themselves poorer than ever, and also, for the first time, forced to leave their homes and their land to fight on the peninsula. In 1866, they revolted and marched on Palermo, but the insurgency was rapidly crushed by the royal navy. Dissatisfaction continued to simmer, often boiling over into small rebellions, and the northern rulers, who viewed the wretched peasants as bandits, imposed martial law.

The economic gap between the industrial north and the poverty-stricken south grew ever wider. Although Sicily was still overwhelmingly agricultural, sulphur had become the island's biggest export. The profits, of course, lined the pockets of the landowners, while the poor, including children as young as six, worked in nightmarish conditions in the mines. By the 1890s, an economic recession crippled Europe, and Sicily's sulphur industry collapsed (although a few mines would limp on until the 1960s). This coincided with a phylloxera blight that decimated the vineyards, and conditions in Sicily became desperate. Sicilians developed their own version of the socialist workers' organizations called *fasci dei lavoratori* that had sprung up on the mainland. The *Fasci Siciliani* demanded land reform and fairer working practices, but, when a peaceful demonstration degenerated into a riot, it was viciously put down and the movement's leaders imprisoned. Emigration began in earnest, as despairing miners and farm labourers left for America and the promise of work: 14,626, around 6% of the island's population, left in 1893 alone. By 1910, more than a million and a half Sicilians (roughly a third of the total population) had emigrated.

Modern Sicily

During the First World War (1914-1918), Sicily was industrialized to some extent in order to provide munitions for the war effort. The organized crime clans known as the Mafia had become increasingly powerful during the last decades of the 19th century and, as well as engaging in extortion, robbery, and murder, they also controlled elections. They were tolerated by the Fascist leader Benito Mussolini until he declared himself dictator in 1925 and no longer required their support: then, he sent in the army to throw anyone suspected of Mafia ties in prison.

Italy allied with Germany during the Second World War (1939-1945) and Sicily was bombed heavily by the Allied powers in preparation for an invasion. The cities, particularly Palermo and Messina, were devastated and thousands of civilians died. Operation Husky, the Allied invasion of Sicily by British, Canadian and American forces, took place in 1943, and the island was quickly subdued. Mussolini was toppled soon after, and Italy's new regime capitulated. The Americans took the western side of the island with little bloodshed, thanks, it is widely believed (although never conclusively proved), to Mafia protection arranged by the American-Sicilian gangster Lucky Luciano. The Mafia also made recommendations for the post-war administrative appointments across the island, instituting a political entrenchment which was cemented when they ensured the victory of the Christian Democrats in the 1948 elections. (The Christian Democrat party was eventually dissolved in 1993, after the government was toppled in a huge corruption scandal and many of its leading politicians were accused of Mafia connections.)

Sicily was granted some autonomy within the Italian republic in 1948, and there was some attempt at land reform. But the promised redistribution of land was a long time coming, and more than 400,000 Sicilians (10% of the population) emigrated between 1951 and 1953. There was a brief boom in the 1950s, when the American Marshall Plan provided funds for reconstruction. Under the massive government programme *Cassa di Mezzogiorno* (Fund for the South), hotels, schools, roads and hospitals were built, and homes provided with electricity. Unfortunately, political corruption and the influence of the Mafia in the construction industry led to shocking abuses, including the (continuing) illegal developments in the supposedly protected Valle dei Templi in Agrigento. Corruption and Mafia-style nepotism remain endemic in almost every area of public life. The Sicilian governor, Salvatore Cuffaro, was found guilty of Mafia collusion in 2008 and forced to resign. Vote-buying remains common practice, and was widely blamed for Cuffaro's victory over the anti-Mafia candidate for governor, Rita Borsellino, in 2006.

Although the crushing poverty of 50 years ago is a thing of the past, Sicily remains one of the 10 poorest regions in the EU, with an unemployment rate of 26% (some observers believe it to be considerably higher). There has been very little investment in agriculture, the fishing industry is declining, and the discovery of oil did not lead to the much-hoped-for boom. Despite this, there is room for cautious optimism. There is slow improvement in the island's infrastructure (the main motorway between Palermo and Messina was finally completed in 2005 after 35 years), gradual renovation of the historical centres of Palermo and Siracusa, and implementation of protected reserves to preserve the island's extraordinary natural heritage. Berlusconi gave the green light to the ambitious and expensive 'Straits of Mesina Bridge' project, which may finally link the island with mainland Sicily. (However, the ousting of Berlusconi and the economic crisis may yet put paid to Sicilian dreams of a closer relationship with the mainland.)

But perhaps most important is the sea change in public opinion towards the Mafia and systemic corruption. The Sicilians, particularly young Sicilians, are refusing to accept the status quo, and are speaking out – unthinkable only a generation ago. The murders of the anti-Mafia magistrates Giovanni Falcone and Paolo Borsellino (brother of Rita) in 1992 shocked the islanders profoundly, and triggered a widespread backlash against the Mafia, with several businesses refusing to pay the *pizzo* (protection money), and popular demonstrations in the streets. Estates confiscated from Mafia members are now being converted into agricultural cooperatives and even *agriturismi*. Tourism is on the increase, and, although emigration is the only option for many Sicilians, several return, often to open the stylish guesthouses and country estates that have become increasingly popular.

When visiting Milan or Rome
Pick up a copy of...
Rome
where
Roman
Rome celebrates 50 years of "Breakfast at Tiffany's" with an exhibition on Audrey Hepburn
Milan
where
wheremilan.com
WELCOME TO THE WORLD DESIGN CAPITAL
Rome
where
wheretraveler.com
Dance with me!
World-class dance festival Equilibrio is back!
Milan
where
CAMPARI
RED PASSION IN MILAN
SHOPPING, DINING, AND ENTERTAINMENT
THIS MONTH EVENTS
wheretraveler.com
where®
MAGAZINE
Local guides. Worldwide

Contents

100 Menu reader

102 Index

Footnotes

Menu reader

General
affumicato smoked
al sangue rare
alla griglia grilled
antipasto starter/appetizer
arrosto roasted
ben cotto well done
bollito boiled
caldo hot
contorni side dishes
coppa/cono cup/cone
cotto cooked
cottura media medium
crudo raw
degustazione tasting menu of several dishes
dolce dessert
fatto in casa homemade
forno a legna wood-fired oven
freddo cold
fresco fresh
fritto fried
piccante spicy
primo first course
ripieno stuffed
secondo second course

Drinks (*bevande*)
acqua naturale/gassata/frizzante still/sparkling water
birra beer
birra (alla spina) beer (draught)
bottiglia bottle
caffè coffee (ie espresso)
caffè macchiato/ristretto espresso with a dash of foamed milk/strong
spremuta freshly squeezed fruit juice
succo juice
vino bianco/rosato/rosso white/rosé/red wine
vin santo a dark, sweet, fortified wine

Fruit (*frutta*) and vegetables (*verdure*)
agrumi citrus fruits
anguria watermelon
arance oranges
carciofio globe artichoke
castagne chestnuts
ciliegie cherries
cipolle onions
fagioli white beans
fichi figs
finocchio fennel
fragole strawberries
funghi mushrooms
lamponi raspberries
legumi pulses
lenticchie lentils
mandorla almond
melagrana pomegranate
melanzana eggplant/aubergine
melone melon
mele apples
noci walnuts
nocciole hazelnuts
patate potatoes, which can be *arroste* (roast), *fritte* (fried), *novelle* (new), *pure' di* (mashed)
peperoncino chilli pepper
peperone peppers
pesche peaches
pinoli pine nuts
piselli peas
pomodori tomato
rucola rocket
spinaci spinach
tartufi truffles
zucca pumpkin

Meat (*carne*)
affettati misti mixed cured meat
agnello lamb
bistecca beef steak
carpaccio finely sliced raw meat (usually beef)
cinghiale wild boar
coda alla vaccinara oxtail
coniglio rabbit
involtini thinly sliced meat, rolled and stuffed
lepre hare
manzo beef
pollo chicken
polpette meatballs
polpettone meat loaf
porchetta roasted, stuffed suckling pig
prosciutto ham – *cotto* cooked, *crudo* cured
salsicce pork sausage
salumi misti cured meats
speck a type of cured, smoked ham
spiedini meat pieces grilled on a skewer
stufato meat stew
trippa tripe
vitello veal

Fish (*pesce*) and seafood (*frutti di mare*)
acciughe anchovies
anguilla eel
aragosta lobster
baccalà salt cod
bottarga mullet-roe
branzino sea bass
calamari squid
cozze mussels

frittura di mare/frittura di paranza small fish, squid and shellfish lightly covered with flour and fried
frutti di mare seafood
gamberi shrimps/prawns
grigliata mista di pesce mixed grilled fish
orata gilt-head/sea bream
ostriche oysters
pesce spada swordfish
polpo octopus
sarde, sardine sardines
seppia cuttlefish
sogliola sole
spigola bass
stoccafisso stockfish
tonno tuna
triglia red mullet
trota trout
vongole clams

Dessert (*dolce*)
cornetto sweet croissant
crema custard
dolce dessert
gelato ice cream
granita flavoured crushed ice
macedonia (di frutta) fruit salad
panettone type of fruit bread eaten at Christmas
semifreddo a partially frozen dessert
sorbetto sorbet
tiramisù rich dessert with cake, cream, coffee and chocolate
torta cake
tozzetti sweet, crunchy almond biscuits
zabaglione whipped egg yolks flavoured with Marsala wine
zuppa inglese trifle

Other
aceto balsamico balsamic vinegar, always from Modena
arborio type of rice used to make risotto
burro butter
calzone folded pizza
formaggi misti mixed cheese plate
formaggio cheese
frittata omelette
insalata salad
insalata Caprese tomatoes, mozzarella and basil
latte milk
miele honey
olio oil
polenta cornmeal
pane bread
pane-integrale brown bread
panzanella bread and tomato salad
provola smoked cheese
ragù a meaty sauce or ragout
riso rice
salsa sauce
sugo sauce or gravy
umbricelli thick spaghetti
zuppa soup

Useful words and phrases
aperitivo a pre-dinner drink, often served with free snacks
posso avere il conto? can I have the bill please?
coperto cover charge
bicchiere glass
c'è un menù? is there a menu?
aperto/chiuso open/closed
prenotazione reservation
conto the bill
cameriere/cameriera waiter/waitress
che cosa mi consegna? what do you recommend?
cos'è questo? what's this?
dov'è il bagno? where's the toilet?

Index → *Entries in bold refer to maps.*

A
accommodation 11-14
  price codes 13
Agrigento 81
  accommodation 86
  directory 87
  festivals and events 87
  restaurants 86
  shopping 87
  transport 87
agriturismi 12
airport information 8
air travel 9
Albergheria, Palermo 25
Alcamo 59
Arbëresh 16

B
Bagheria 43
Bourbon Sicily 94
bus/coach travel 9, 11

C
Caccamo 45
Cala (La), Palermo 30
Cappella Palatina, Palermo 25
car hire 10
Carnevale 16
Casa Natale di Luigi Pirandello, Agrigento 83
Castelbuono 47
Castel di Tusa 47
Castellammare del Golfo 58
Castello della Zisa, Palermo 34
Castello Incantato 85
Cattedrale di Monreale 43
Cattedrale di San Gerlando, Agrigento 83
Cattedrale, Palermo 28
Cefalù 45
  accommodation 49
  beaches 47
  directory 54
  entertainment 52
  festivals and events 52
  restaurants 51
  shopping 53
  transport 54
Chiesa del Gesù, Palermo 25
Chiesa della Martorana, Palermo 29
Chiesa del Purgatorio 63
Chiesa di San Cataldo, Palermo 29
Chiesa di San Domenico, Palermo 32
Chiesa di San Francesco d'Assisi, Palermo 32
Chiesa di San Giovanni, Marsala 73
Chiesa di San Nicolò all'Albergheria, Palermo 25
Chiesa di Santa Maria dei Greci, Agrigento 83
Chiesa di Santa Maria dei Miracoli, Palermo 30
Chiesa di Santa Maria del Carmine, Palermo 25
Chiesa di Santa Maria della Catena, Palermo 30
Christianity 93
Città vecchia, Cefalù 46
Collesano 47
Complesso San Pietro, Museo Garibaldino, Marsala 73
Convento dei Cappuccini, Palermo 35
cooking classes 40, 53

Corleone 42
Corso Vittorio Emanuele, Palermo 28
Couscous Fest 17
cuisine 14, 14-16
  menu reader 100
customs 19
cycling 11

D
diving 53, 64, 69
Duomo
  Cefalù 45
  Marsala 73

E
Easter 17
eating price codes 13
Egadi Islands, The 66
  accommodation 68
  festivals and events 69
  restaurants 68
  transport 69
emergency numbers 19
entertainment 69
Eraclea Minoa 84
Erice 58
essentials 19-21
Estate a Marsala 78
etiquette 19

F
Falconara 83
Favara 83
Favignana
  directory 70
Favignana, Egadi Islands 66
Festa del Mandorlo 16
Festa di Maria SS del Lume 17
Festa Nazionale della Befana 16

102 • Footnotes Index

Festino di Santa Rosalia 17, 39
festivals 16-18
food and drink 14-16
  menu reader 100
  price codes 13
Foro Italico, Palermo 32

G
Galleria di Arte Moderna e Restivo, Palermo 30
Galleria Regionale della Sicilia, Palermo 30
Gela 83
Giardino di Garibaldi, Palermo 30
Giardino Inglese, Palermo 34
Gibellina Nuovo 76
Grotto del Genovese, Levanzo 66
Grotto dell'Addaura 42
Grotto of the Sibyl, Marsala 73

H
health 19
Himera 44
history 90
hotels 12

I
Il Capo, Palermo 33
Il Pellegrinaggio alla Madonna del Tindari 17
I Misteri di Trapani 63
Isola di San Pantoleo 60
Italian Unification 94

K
Kalsa (La), Palermo 30
Kals'Art festival 39

L
Levanzo, Egadi Islands 66
Licata 83

Luglio Musicale Trapanese 63

M
Madonie 47
  accommodation 49
  festivals and events 52
  restaurants 51
  shopping 53
  transport 54
Manfria 83
Marettimo, Egadi Islands 66
Marina di Palma 83
Marsala 73
  accommodation 77
  directory 79
  entertainment 78
  festivals and events 78
  restaurants 77
  shopping 78
  transport 79
  what to do 78
Mattanza 69
Mazara del Vallo 74
Medieval Sicily 93
menu reader 100
Mercato del Capo, Palermo 33
Mercato della Vucciria, Palermo 32
Modern Sicily 96
Monastero di Santo Spirito, Agrigento 83
Mondello 42
money 20
Monte Pellegrino 42
Mozia 60
Museo Archeologico Baglio Anselmi, Marsala 73
Museo Archeologico Regionale Salinas, Palermo 33
Museo con gli Arazzi Fiamminghi, Marsala 73

Museo d'Arte Contemporanea della Sicilia, Palermo 29
Museo Diocesano, Palermo 28
Museo Internazionale delle Marionette Antonio Pasqualino, Palermo 30
Museo Mandralisca, Cefalù 46
Museo Regionale Archeologico, Agrigento 82
Museo Regionale Pepoli, Trapani 57

N
Naro 83

O
Oasi WWF di Torre Salsa 84
opening hours 20
Oratorio del Rosario di San Domenico, Palermo 33
Oratorio di San Lorenzo, Palermo 32
Oratorio di Santa Zita, Palermo 33

P
Palazzo Asmundo, Palermo 28
Palazzo dei Normanni, Palermo 25
Palazzo Mirto, Palermo 30
Palermo 24, **27**
  accommodation 36
  directory 40
  entertainment 38
  festivals and events 39
  outskirts 34
  restaurants 37
  shopping 39
  transport 40
  what to do 40

Palermo Estate and Verdura Festival 17
Pantelleria 67
  accommodation 68
  restaurants 68
  shopping 69
  transport 69
  what to do 69
Parco della Favorita, Palermo 35
Parco delle Madonie 47
Petralia Soprana 47
Petralia Sottana 47
Piana degli Albanesi 42
Piano Battaglia 47
Piazza Bellini, Palermo 29
Piazza Marina, Palermo 30
piazza Repubblica, Marsala 73
Piazza Ruggero Settimo, Palermo 34
police 20
Porta Felice, Palermo 32
Porto Empedocle 83
post 20
Presepi di Natale 18
price codes 13

Q
Quattro Canti, Palermo 28, 29

R
rail travel 10
Rappresentazioni Pirandelliane, 87
restaurants 15
Riserva Naturale dello Zingaro 59
road travel 9, 10
Rocca (La), Cefalù 46

Roman and Byzantine Sicily 92
Ruderi di Gibellina 76

S
safety 20
Salemi 76
Santa Margherita di Belice 75
Santuario dell'Annunziata, Trapani 57
Santuario di Gibilmanna 47
San Vito Lo Capo 59
Scala dei Turchi 83
Sciacca 84
Scopello 59
sea travel 9, 11
Segesta 59
Selinunte 74
Siculiana 83
sleeping price codes 13
Soluntо 44
Southwestern Sicily 71-88
  overview 6
Spanish rule 94

T
Teatro Massimo, Palermo 34
Teatro Pirandello, Agrigento 83
Termini Imerese 44
tipping 21
tourist information 21
transport 8-11
  air 8, 9
  airport information 8
  bicycle 11
  bus/coach 9, 11
  car hire 10
  ferry 9, 11

  rail 10
  road 9, 10
  sea 9, 11
Trapani 57
  accommodation 62
  directory 64
  festivals and events 63
  restaurants 62
  shopping 64
  transport 64
  what to do 64
Tutti i Santi (All Saints' Day) 18

U
Ustica 47
  accommodation 50
  directory 54
  transport 54
  what to do 53

V
Valle dei Templi, Agrigento 81
Via del Sale 60
via Libertà, Palermo 34
Villa Malfitano, Palermo 35
Villa Palagonia, Bagheria 44
Vulcanelli di Maccalube 83

W
Western Sicily 55-70
  overview 6
where to stay 11-14
  price codes 13
wine 15, 53, 64, 69, 78, 79

Z
Zampogna d'Oro 63